SHARED MOMENTS

Edited by

Zoë Rock

First published in Great Britain in 2000 by
POETRY NOW
Remus House,
Coltsfoot Drive,
Peterborough, PE2 9JX
Telephone (01733) 898101
Fax (01733) 313524

HB ISBN 0 75432 491 5
SB ISBN 0 75432 492 3

FOREWORD

Although we are a nation of poets we are accused of not reading poetry, or buying poetry books. After many years of listening to the incessant gripes of poetry publishers, I can only assume that the books they publish, in general, are books that most people do not want to read.

Poetry should not be obscure, introverted, and as cryptic as a crossword puzzle: it is the poet's duty to reach out and embrace the world.

The world owes the poet nothing and we should not be expected to dig and delve into a rambling discourse searching for some inner meaning.

The reason we write poetry (and almost all of us do) is because we want to communicate: an ideal; an idea; or a specific feeling. Poetry is as essential in communication, as a letter; a radio; a telephone, and the main criterion for selecting the poems in this anthology is very simple: they communicate.

CONTENTS

RUSSIA NIGHT

I found a niche, indisputable
'mongst masses of like-minded,
optimistic souls.
Every mauve shadow, every echo
whispered day, breathed promise.
I saw the baton lift, live, mystique,
a wand, spirited, spry
hold piebald pageantry of note;
the Volga seeped through
my consciousness;
black and red, Tchaikovsky's
fluent flaunting, sweetening sound;
rippling ebony concerto tone,
fanatical, febrile, excelled.
Richer that I had ever been
I tangled with torrents,
tempestuousness of tune.
Rimsky-Korsakov, rampant, royal,
regaled the avid dream with light.
Rachmaninov surprised,
revolutionised incredulity,
made magic mightily a monarch,
master of my senses,
mistress of my mind.
All Russia revelled, breathing fire;
demons dared delight return;
again and yet again I rollicked,
rolled with drum, choked
and, on cello's chocolate charm
capitulated.

Ruth Daviat

DREAMS

Fear has no place here, neither
Doubt, nor shame, nor death.
I am very much alive, though
Not awake. Just drifting till morn,
Drawing strength with every breath.
Faces new and faces old, enmesh
Themselves and become one, friend or foe
Eyes can't discern, yet no harm
Will come. The script is mine
To tell. It will be so.
It is my special time, the night,
When sleep refreshes me with dreams
Of fantastic images painted on
The insides of my eyelids, so
Nothing is as it seems.
Clocks bear no intrusion here, hour
Hands play silent on cloudy dials.
No time to call on the dream
Stories' fate. Forgotten frowns
Usurped by morning smiles.
How then can I favour so much, this
Time, each dream, each hazy night,
When often I remember not how I
Spent the hours behind closed eyes,
Unrecognised in fresh daylight?
It is because I have the chance,
The power to create moments, new
And unreal. To change, to relive
This worn out life. And it is
Because I can dream of you.

Frances Pallett

CHILDHOOD DAYS

There never was such freedom
As in those childhood days,
How innocent we were then
In all our different ways.

Some of those years were wartime
But we didn't know the pain,
We knew that fathers went away
We hoped they'd come again.

But from that Shropshire village
The war seemed far away,
We youngsters roamed the countryside
And no one told us 'Nay'.

We played, we biked, we rambled,
Sailed paper boats and fished,
Ran along with the harvester
To kill rabbits, which we missed!

We played in fields and copses
A tree house too was ours,
There was nothing that we couldn't do
- We picked the squire's flowers

And took them home to mothers
So's they wouldn't cuff our ears
Because our clothes were torn and dirty,
And we knew there might be tears!

We went scrumping squire's windfalls
When he was out for the day,
We'd dig in the woods for pig nuts
And eat them in the hay.

O happy childhood memories
They'll never fade away.

Joan Marsh

A New Day

Leaves tumble down in the wake of the wind
Seagulls soar high as their new day begins.
Clouds move along on the breath of a breeze
The sun casting hues orange, pink and cerise.

The frosty dawn air tingles my nose
Gloves keep my hands warm, wellies my toes.
And as I wander 'neath autumn-torn trees
Hear the crisp, crunchy, crackle of trodden-on leaves.

The new day is quiet, the stillness around
No railway rumbles, no siren sounds.
Two magpies sit at the top of a tree
Watching the progress of my dog and me.

From tree trunk to tree trunk, from bushes to fence,
Tail wagging wildly, another new scent.
Ears pointed upwards, nose to the ground
Snuffling and snorting, now what's he found?

How many people this beauty behold
They walk with their eyes down, no light in their soul.
How many look around them and see
The wonders of nature that surround me.

Beth Gardiner

THE OLD HOUSE

The old house stands forlorn, crumbling,
Wind and weather increasingly taking their toll,
Birds confidently raise countless families, in ravaged brickwork.
In leaking, broken guttering, wild flowers bloom profusely
Almost ringing the house like a halo,
Their beauty and brightness belie their station,
Two chimney stacks still stand tall and proud
Like sentinels on special duty,
Rotting windows like sightless eyes
Stare upon an unchanging view,
A door hangs drunkenly, swaying and groaning in the wind,
Now incapable of protecting a once welcoming threshold,
Many lives were nurtured within these walls,
Happiness, sadness, new life, and death.
All unravelled their complexities here,
Now life's game is played out, only the props survive,
Someday soon only memories will remain.

Barbara L Jones

A Special Caring And Sharing

Time slips away, I stand alone in dappled
light, until an errant breeze emboldens me
towards the Hall, so festive, bright and
filling with a multitude. I join the throng,
in evening's golden softness, lingering
the mellowness, someone shakes my hand.
  Welcome warms me in a colourful embrace of
  parents, youthful, happy with their first
  born, his birth, our celebration, my own
  eyes mist, remember the girl next door,
  now wife and mother, greeting guests who've
  travelled from afar, new seeds of friendship sown.
Fragrance wafts the spicy courses, succulent
and hot, so redolent of lives we've left behind,
desserts of creamy fruit, with love cooked
into every stage of preparation, carefully
transported, served with icy drinks,
crisp salads, no preference overlooked.
  The baby cries, then settles into new clothes
  trimmed with gold, specially sent by
  relatives across the seas, the tiny guest
  of honour, reigning in his motley court.
  His family, friends and neighbours most formally
  arrayed, give him their best, from east and west.
In sunset's technicolour blaze, we are as one,
in interfaith, gathered in this Hall of the Good
Shepherd, caring, sharing the Hakika, goodwill,
love and peace, in all our hearts. Then cameras
flash, the music fades farewell and I walk alone
in coolness, shadowing images when time stood still.

Lorna Troop

THE NURSERY

They stood around the gate, mouths
still and eyes open to strangeness,
Stranger to them but not to her:
So little, so special, so joyful.

Told about him they saw the wonder
and the selfless love, the smiles and hugs,
She felt she was special and knew
and felt want and wishing given.

Helped and climbing into the
place that takes them home,
She stares at friendship scattered,
And heeds her mother's heeding.

Movement stalls, he looks around,
And stretches, moving webbing clear,
Grasping little fingers, eyes meet,
And joy exchanged forever.

M J Pickthall

THE SIMPLE LIFE

Oh, for those simple days which ran slower!
Playing card games by the light and warmth of the fire
While Mother would be knitting,
Sitting in Father's rocking chair.
Then cuddled round her, listening as she read to us
Stories like 'The Hobbit' or 'Swallows and Amazons'
Or in summer swimming in local ponds or beaches,
Sailing in our boat, roving where the wind took us
Then fishing for our supper.
Exploring the straight Roman roads or bending, country lanes,
Delighting in the countryside's colours,
Glimpsing above the old hedges horses and their riders,
Enjoying the unhurried tempo and freedom of life.
Farmers abiding by Nature's laws but helping when they could,
Especially their flocks and herds at birthing time,
Harvesting the bountiful fields and fruits,
Farmyards full of noisy geese, ducks and hens,
Cats chasing or lying under the glorious sun.
Oh, those days of fun when everything seemed big to us
With life drifting along at its leisurely pace.

Tilla B Smith

GEORGIANA REBEKAH

Skin on skin and eyes to eyes
The moment we first met
This tiny baby with skin so soft
To love, cherish and protect

How could such a tiny body
Have such big hands and feet?
How could such a loud noise
Be coming from someone so sweet?

Big blue eyes so beautiful
Not a ginger hair in sight!
A little girl so wonderful
She fills all with delight

The difficult struggle and lengthy birth
All forgotten on the double
As we touched with infinite tenderness
That was our first cuddle

Karen Naylor

MY SPECIAL HOBBIES

My special hobbies are poetry and art
They express the thoughts that come from my heart
Both talents were born in times of great sadness
But over the years have brought such gladness.
An operation, then the death of my dad,
A broken marriage, they left me so sad.
Then I started to express the thoughts in my mind
With pencil and pen, serenity I would find.
A sad little poem when I am feeling blue,
Painting a stormy sea expresses it too.
A beautiful sunset or a snowy winter scene
A poem telling how good life has been.
The joy from my grandchildren put into rhyme
Holiday paintings, memories forged for all time.
These are the things that give me such pleasure
Life has a purpose, and joy beyond measure.

Lynne Walden

PRECIOUS MOMENTS

I have had many precious moments in my life
I remember the day I became a wife
The following year when I became a mother
Then two years later when there was a baby brother
This pattern was repeated two times more
So now we had a lovely family of four.
There were so many precious times now to recall
That it would be too difficult to count them all.
On reflection what you remember over the years
Are the special happy times and not the traumas and tears.
Now that I'm a granny the special times come frequently
Just cuddling each new baby or giving older ones their tea
I had a happy childhood myself so I have those memories too
Recorded in photo albums which are great fun to look through.
I know that I've been lucky as my precious moments are many
Lots of other people perhaps do not have any.
I thank God for my family who are so good to me
They sent me and my hubby to Rome quite recently
So thanks for the memories which we still can share
Of the special occasions we have with those who care.

Mary Anne Scott

MY MUM

I shall never forget my mum
For her voice I still hear each day
The many things she did for me
In her own sweet loving way
She gave me years of happiness
Her smile was like a breath of spring
Her heart was pure as gold
For she left me with so many memories
To treasure through the years to come
For she was my mum and best friend too

Ella Wright

COASTAL FOG

Hear the sound of the hooter
As it plays its warning cheer,
Helping boats on our waters
When the elements are not clear.

See the dim lights of danger
As they go sailing closely by,
Hear the sound as it travels
Over land and sea and sky.

Risk is for the taking
And is shaped by one and all
As the people that are sailing
Can so easily recall

Les J Croft

HISTORY - MADE OR MAKING

This sense of history can be intense.
If we have acquired an historical sense
Visiting Egypt, to be awed by pyramidal power
Or in Luxor where gigantic pillars tower.
Still amaze, how ancient stones were carried and carved
While millions laboured hard, sometimes starved.

When younger - the immense drama of the Normandy landing.
Millions of us - involved in a gigantic battle
Seen from the deck of a ship - as landing craft were grounding
To the boom of naval guns and machine guns' rattle.
All of us, torn by fears and the discipline of naval codes
Conscious of Europe over which the Nazis ruled.

Every city inspires a page of history, in Britain Plymouth.
Linked with all the legends of our naval past.
Dover - Dunkirk and towns at rivers' mouth.
Paris - Berlin - Moscow gigantic plays where millions were in the cast.
All the world is a stage, we see only a few scenes
But it is important. To know we are the players.

Dave Davis

CHILDHOOD REMEMBERED IN LEEDS

Our world was full of things to do our playground streets and parks
Rides on our bikes to Gledhow Valley, where we played many a lark
Kick-out-can on Gathorne Terrace, Potty Park was hide and seek
In the woods of Gledhow Valley running thru' pipes that leak
Our old bikes took us everywhere, we roamed far and wide
But always had some jam and bread and water by our side
The Gaiety was thought quite nice, Harehills bug hutch the worse
To the Clock you went with Mother and sat quiet without a curse
To the town we'd travel often, the Empire was just grand
Myself and Mary Irving would sit listening to the band
The Gallery was the cheapest to see Dickie Valentine and swoon
With Joseph Locke and Alma Cogan we passed many an afternoon

The snow brought added pleasure I used to go quite mad
Racing down the hillside on a sledge made by my dad
Roundhay Park was our favourite, Hill 60 was the best
My sledge could slide like lightning as I tried to beat the rest

Memories I have of years ago of days not long enough
Though we were never full of woe yet times were often tough
One thing we never had or missed or needed at that time
Was money which was very scarce but nobody had a dime
Dwelling on the things we did we never had to fear
Nobody ever bothered us as we wandered far and near
We felt such great excitement at everything we did
The streets seemed full of things to do when I was just a kid!

F Newlands-Du'Barry

BUTTERFLY

Like woven white silk paper thin in texture
Your wings flutter against a sudden gust of wind
Almost as gentle and as fluid frail as a sweet dream
You with your delicate winged veins upon the garden wall
Lands somewhere into the middle of my life
Slicing the seconds of peaceful reflection forever
You visit me in the mess of dark mind dark thought
Just being beautiful and brief amongst man's science
In the middle of man's reality and conceited world
Bees will hum the summer months into their honey
And I in crude comparison will eat of their labour
Likewise I will eat away at your beauty which you spill freely
Consume its essence so that I might look upon it long after your
                                        absence from this life
Along the garden path you flutter your wings in goodbye
And the motion of these white petals of propulsion
Fade into the afternoon leaving me empty and alone.

Christine Denise Wells

CORNWALL

We strayed from white-washed cottages,
and the great stone harbour wall,
along a narrow beach, beyond upstanding rocks,
the five of us, Mum and Dad,
and three young kids, together,
all in off-peak gear,
breathing briny air.

Across some half-forgotten bay,
deserted open surface up for grabs,
we stretched a long thin caravan,
and vowed we'd stay forever,
cradled in strong arms,
lulled to sleep,
by the murmur of the sea.

But even as we stood there,
gazing out across the shining sand,
time slipped through the screeching gulls and breaking waves,
and dropped a summons at our feet,
returning us to well-known avenues,
along familiar routes,
home.

And now the roar of city traffic thunders round
deaf ears. Fumes seep through blocked pores.
Urgent files crammed in a leather case,
with half a million tired commuting souls,
leave just a scrap of room,
for holidays in Cornwall,
the waving grasses round a granite tomb.

A K S Shaw

INDESTRUCTIBLE

In the grips of the severest form
of chemotherapy,
my fantastic mum amazes me.

Referring to the love she's shown
by her adoring family,
she beams at me and speaks
from the bottom of her heart -

'I must be the luckiest woman in the world.'

What kind of joy is that?
The kind I will never forget.

Jeanne Hutton

THE MIKADO

What fun we had as we practised so hard
the opera Mikado at school, singing in music
lessons and staying after school with a sandwich
and a drink.
Every one of us was so keen, from us the chosen
children of thirteen to fifteen, to the teachers,
headmistress and headmaster, it was a joint school
for girls and boys you see.
It was dress rehearsal, on went the yellow make-up
that felt like pancake on our faces. Did we
laugh as we looked at each other, but we really
looked the part.
Then came the great day of curtain up for
all the families, friends and public not forgetting
the Mayor and Mayoress.
All said after each performance, 'What a splendid
evening we have had, really enjoyed it, the singing
for school children so good.'
Then came the invite from the Mayor to stage
the opera at the Town Hall, the headmaster and
headmistress and our parents so proud of us.
I look back very often at that special time
in my young life.

G H Pocock

CHRISTMAS EVE PARTY

Tonight was Christmas Eve, party time in the parish hall.
On arrival a soft covering of powdered snow fell delicately all around.
Each window shone with an assortment of lovely hand-crafted
paper chains.
The door appeared smaller than usual, as a huge Christmas tree
stretched from the floor to the ceiling.
Sporting colossal outstretched branches, heavily laden with baubles,
crepe ribbons, tinsel, streamers and holly.
Hundreds of fairy lights created a kaleidoscope of colour,
across the open car park.
Golden bells tinkled, as one tried to squeeze past congregating adults.
Inside peals of laughter and merriment rose steadily as the games got
underway.
Coins rattled into biscuit tins, a shilling a go to throw bean bags.
Sixpence for throwing rubber rings onto a number board.
My favourite, two shillings and sixpence a go for the train raffle.
Tonight I had the winning ticket, number four hundred and five.
My prize, six highly painted glazed egg cups, donated by Aunt Rene.
Rice crispy buns, iced queen cakes and orange juice for children.
Mince pies, Christmas cake, tea and coffee for parents,
Served by ladies in small crisp white aprons.
Suddenly my eye caught a glimpse of something red.
A huge Father Christmas sat, smiling and talking happily to lots of
small children
Between large mouthfuls of Christmas cake and steaming hot tea
Promising surprise gifts for all on Christmas morning.
At the end of a long night, little girls and boys clung impatiently
to their parents' clothing.
Little girls in expensive party dresses and fancy hair clips,
Adorned with colourful jewellery, beads, bangles, brooches,
rings and earrings.

Small boys with neat haircuts, dressed in Sunday best.
Each one in turn, had behaved like an angel in front of their parents
and grandparents alike.
Starry-eyed and totally amazed, my very first Christmas party,
at the age of four in the parish hall.

Linda White

A SPECIAL WEDDING

Best wishes and love
To you both today.
May the future prove,
Both in work and in play,
You will keep in mind
The gift to be kind.

Though you may feel fraught,
Seek fulfilment to share;
Perception and thought
Are enriching and rare;
Long may you live
To care and to give.

Communicate and discuss
Worries, cares and fears,
Eliminate fuss,
Accept laughter and tears,
Cherish commitment for life
As husband and wife.

S J Dodwell

HOLIDAY IN HEMSBY

Hemsby sands,
kissed by the sea.
Once visited,
by my family and me.
We walked the beaches,
in the bright June sun.
Climbed the sand dunes
just for fun.
Spent time in the arcades,
purchased souvenirs and postcards.
Relations from south Norfolk,
offered us their kind regards.
A walk into Hemsby village,
camera clicking all the while.
Collecting the cherished memories,
that would later make us smile.
Saint Mary the virgin Hemsby,
tower reaching for the sky.
Photographed from all angles,
a treat for the human eye.
The beach road to Newport,
on a hill the beach shop.
After a day in Hemsby,
this would be our last stop.
Then back to the caravan,
to pass the night away.
The family excited by the prospect,
of the events of the new day.

M A Challis

A BEAKERFUL OF MEMORIES

In this delicious beaker
Of frothy malted milk
Are memories of beaches
Seen by an eager child
On long-awaited holidays;
Also of childish smiles and tensions,
Victories, defeats.

Home-goings I deplored.
But there was always next year,
And the sea would still be there!
And thus life would continue . . .

Then childhood turned its back!
And took with it that charm,
Unique and irretrievable,
Which beaches hold for those whose years
Are only very few.

Dora Hawkins

INTO AUTUMN

The needs of life are gentler
Our youthful dreams are made
And morning comes more slowly
As night-time shadows fade

A softer feeling joins us now
Released from heady passion
In the ever-changing patterns
Of pathways we have fashioned

Our offspring grew and blossomed
Obligations were fulfilled
The cord now neatly severed
Their echoes linger still

Fond memories of summer, turn
To autumn skies above
And we can quietly contemplate
This misused word called 'love'

Sylvia Partridge

FIRST MATE

I really am proud and I appreciate,
To have you dear for my first mate,
So welcome aboard the good ship
'Enterprise'
The world is our oyster,
Let us reach for the skies,
We will sail these stormy seas together,
No matter what the wind or weather,
Our life Darling has just begun,
Let us live it and have lots of fun,
No doubt we will travel many miles,
Enriched of course by your sweet smiles,
You and I will enjoy this life,
'Cause someday soon you will be my wife,
To have and to hold eternally,
And happy we shall ever be.
When our travelling days are over,
Together we shall be in clover,
Our thoughts and our eternal love,
Whenever you think of the future,
Whenever you think of me,
I hope we will do it together,
Where e'er on the sphere we may be,
And live our lives together - eternally,
Everlasting, forever, without end.

Jim McGlade

WHAT!

Voluptuous colour, iridescent sheen,
Warm to feel, finger stroke, to dream,
Warm sunshine on a dappled wooded stroll,
Meandering by the sparkled rippling stream,
Arms entwined, bodies close, a juicy kiss,
Dainty flowers, peeping through elegant straight grasses,
Dancing butterflies, buzzing bees, gliding dragonfly,
Birdsong trilling through the lacy leaves,
Dancing in the gentle breeze,
Melodious, sublime, love divine,
Colour fills the scene, voluptuous fruits
Of the early peeping seedling, romance,
So the sweet fruits of summer, heart's delight,
Ripening, softening in the all-embracing sunshine,
Hence the richness of the precious 'ruby'
Has been chosen for years of wedded union,
Gazing into its voluptuous redness, there
Is no bottom sighted in this glorious stone,
Just the eternal warmth of love,
So we serenade the happiness bubbling
In the hearts of our happy couple,
As bubbling as the champagne sparkle,
In our crystal glasses,
Good marriages sure are made in Heaven
Blessed with the hand of God,
Through all the ups and downs of life,
May your years be many more.

Anne Mary McMullan

FOR MY BEST FRIEND

We meet people every day
As we live our busy lives
And friendships form along the way
Which will or won't survive.

But you stood out from all the rest
And when I wonder why
I realise as friends we're the best
Because we don't have to try

There is no lie, nothing false or strained
In things we say or do
Upon each other we can depend
To each other be always true

If I want to cry or laugh or talk
You'll always lend an ear
If you need a hug or go for a walk
You know I'm always near

That's what makes us the best of friends
The fact that it's not just me or you
But we know that right to the very end
It'll be you and me, me and you.

Sarah Gibbs

FIRST MEETING

The blip a mesmerising point of light -
a firefly undulating on the screen -
I watched your progress down the homeward straight
and monitored that steady, pulsing gleam.

The wires between a coded thought-exchange -
a flash of semaphore, a stab of pain
answering, my signals urged you on,
anticipation flooding every vein.

Blood rhythms beat a high-pitched, throbbing song,
my breathless chorus rising as you neared,
and agony and ecstasy were one
as you arrived and everybody cheered.

The moment burst upon us in a blur
of sheer sensation - physical and deep -
and rapture shook me, laughing through my tears,
amazed that joy so fierce could make me weep.

J M Harvey

ON EARTH

September, month of change, the grass is tired, dull beige.
Leaves carpet the mossy earth.
It's warm and then not.
Parthenosis blushes at the rogue honeysuckle
Taking liberties with the warm wall.

September brings a mellow brightness, tiger streaks of light.
Golden rod, teasels, orange hips - broom pods pop.
Blackberries squash between fingers and tongues.
Small birds feast on hung nuts and
Squirrels make a tree-line dash.

Spiders are not the only inhabitants of webs
We too have become part of a wider net
Held together by a world of wire and
Signals moving in any direction
At a click.

Our mouse works hard
And how trying when all crashes
Like the fragile web
In the michaelmas daisies
With its stripped incumbent.

Janet Farley

DAY AWAY

Simple days of bucket
     and spade -
Ice-cream cornets,
     lemonade.

Carefree childhood -
     day away!
A little girl got
     lost today.

Funfair rides on
     roundabout,
Smiling faces as they
     shout -

'Mummy, Daddy - look
     it's me!
I'm on the fire engine
     don't you see?'

Clang the bell -
     another ride!
Choose the bus - we'll
     go inside.

Such a lovely day
     away -
We'll come again
     another day!

Bracing air - so
     fresh and free -
Friendly Skegness -
     by the sea!

Mary Skelton

MY BABY MICHAEL
(Dedicated to my newborn baby Michael)

My magic moment,
The birth of my baby son Michael,
He is so cute and looks like me,
I'm so proud and delighted,
Me, Michelle Knight, a mother,
My mum Christine, who's in Heaven,
Would be proud of me,
She would have been a grandma,
My baby son Michael my first child,
He was born on Saturday, 19th August 2000,
He was born at 1.30am,
He was born at The City Hospital,
Winson Green, Birmingham,
His full name is,
Michael Apollo Ronan Chakotay Knight,
It's such a delight to be a mother,
I couldn't believe I was a mum,
It's an amazing experience,
I will now be a good mother to my son Michael,
Years of fun and experiences to look forward to,
He's such a delight, a little darling,
Everybody likes him,
I've had a lot of praise and congratulations,
Now the hard work starts,
To bring him up the best I can,
To give him all I had and never had,
I will tell him about his Grandma Christine,
He has brown hair, brown eyes,
I am happy and delighted,
Me, Michelle, the mother of Michael Knight.

Michelle Knight

TOGETHER AT CHRISTMAS

Christmas Eve has passed and gone
Christmas Day has just begun
Outside it's cold and brisk
No sign of early morning mist

Inside the fire's burning bright
Giving out its glowing warmth
Candles on the mantelpiece giving out their glow
Christmas is special, that we know

My family will soon arrive
Then things will soon be in full swing
Then let the party now begin
Christmas is special, that's for sure
And being surrounded by family
I couldn't ask for more.

Janet Hannan

THE ONE I LOVE

(Dedicated to my husband Keith Christian . . . the one who
I want to grow old with and prune the roses together)

I think of you every day,
I'm so glad you came my way
To love and cherish what we have,
Then this world doesn't feel so bad

Our love is there to nurture and feed,
Just like a growing seed
To take the good with the bad,
Every day I feel so glad
To have you in my life,
I feel so proud to be your wife.

Sharon Christian

BRIEF ENCOUNTER
(Dedicated to Curly)

Whilst walking through a busy crowd,
The single figure stood defined and proud;
This dutiful wife and loving mother,
Old hopes and dreams now belong to another.
Connected stare over checkout counter,
This Mall, this stage of a brief encounter,
She tarried by signs in the local grocer,
Unspoken word, to beckon come closer;
Is that your Self? Asked I so careful,
As not to annoy and be so wareful.
Kind words and gestures were both exchanged,
My fears and doubts over years have changed;
Like phantoms of the past quickly seen and gone,
Both laid to rest may our lives move on;
Questions answered at a checkout counter,
Closing the page on a brief encounter.

Andrew Bray

THE TREE OF LIFE

The gnarled short fat tree trunk lay on the
golden sand,
I had my ancient Brownie box camera in my
hand.

My daughter sat upon the dark brown bark,
looking so nervous just as though she had
seen a large shark.

I took the birthday photograph it was part
of a set,
they grow up so quickly you need moments
that you'd not want to forget.

For like the sea that changes the whole
shape of our land,
Nature changes children till they let go
of your hand and turn into something
that is of quite another brand.

As none of us are clones of our people
in the past,
I bet if they all saw us now they'd
really be aghast.

Jean Paisley

THE LETHAL LEGACY

And so they came -
Now at last it seemed so right
Never before such affinity, when
At last we met that late, late night.
A vision of loveliness and joy were they,
Never doubting our welcome and our love
Distanced from that lethal nuclear legacy,
Keeping their lungs clean with our air,
And building immune systems still.
Those 'straws in the wind', helpless and ill,
Errors of man caused Chernobyl's spill
Remembering now the words of one -
'I try so hard to make you love me'
No need to try, our hearts are won,
And so they left, far over the seas.

Mary C Armstrong

MEMORIES ON ARTHUR'S SEAT

The eagle soars over the mountainous magnitude
That eradicates the sun from my soul.
And the still earth listens, as the footsteps fall
On the green, lush dress of her youth.
The mist swirls over the glen,
And her eyes fill with unshed tears.
Glazing over the rocky expanse
To the ruined fortress of a once known love
Memories, hazy like the dew of dawn
Remembering love tender, touch light.
Like the breeze caressing my arms at night.
A knowledge of something once known.
Tangible, yet out of sight.
As I gaze again to the hills,
And the lonely eagle in flight.
I wonder if he sees her as I,
If he feels passion or death in his flight?

Cate Campbell

THE SEA

Is it blue? Or is it green?
One of the prettiest sights to be seen.
The tide rushes in and waves rush out
Throwing the pebbles around and about
Lives can be lost in a stormy air
Also laps at the shore in the swimmer's glare
Fast launches flying in a heavy spray
Fishermen working from night 'til day
Red flags are blowing, swimmers beware
Children playing, they haven't a care
Bodies lying in the midday sun
The beach is crowded with everyone.
Yachts pass by with their sails so bright
Big ships thunder past in the dead of night
Ferries rushing to and fro
Off to France, look, see them go,
A leisurely walk along the foreshore
People keep coming back for more
A game of chance in the amusement arcade
Go in, out of the sun, into the shade.
Buckets and spades and the slimy rock pools
To miss these sights, you must be fools
Is it blue? Or is it green?
Must be the prettiest sight you've ever seen.

Muriel Turner

SPECIAL THINGS IN MY LIFE

I met my husband nineteen years ago,
But it only seems like yesterday.
I love him lots and lots and lots,
I think our love still has the hots.

We've had many, many happy times,
Like the birth of our children that were all fine.
A lovely home that's his and mind,
Two good dogs that protect all the time.

My Grandad lives just next door,
He gives us love and more and more.
My mum and Tim come most days,
The children love them all to play.

The life I have is just great,
I would not change it in anyway.
My children are the light of my life,
The best thing is being a mum and a wife.

Dee Dickens

A TIME TO CARE

Surely every minute of every day,
Is a special time for someone,
Somebody, somewhere will remember,
Today for special reasons,
They will look back and say,
Yes that was my special day,
Building their lives,
Around the memory,
Of that special time,
So all time is special,
A second never passes,
Without being cherished,
By someone, somewhere,
A time to savour,
A time to care.

P J Littlefield

KYLIE'S STAIRWAY TO HEAVEN

(To Kylie, whose memory deserves to be set in gold and to her brother
Steven John Woods, whose heart of gold keeps her memory alive each
and every day, and to Sheila, their mum, for giving them life.)

A life that is so beautiful that does deserve to live
That giveth all she has to us and makes us want to give
A face so filled with loving and every bit of hope
A life so filled with everything and now it's hard to cope
'Cause now she's gone to heaven the angels called her name
They needed her to cherish the little ones who came
Up to the mystic heavens and by God's side she stands
And all the little angels put out their little hands
And welcomed little Kylie they took her by the arm
And led her to the stairway where there was no more harm
And now that you do miss her and wish her back with you
Please think of all the suffering she never will go through
Please think of your sweet sister as she did look that day
And put your hands together and on this day do pray
That Kylie will be watching that she will look on down
And see you smiling up there an ever silent sound
'Cause Kylie is an angel she's loved by everyone
And now she is God's helper and lives up in the sun
Her presence ever glowing her life was so worthwhile
'Cause she will be remembered with the most beautiful smile
And on her soul will live now another part of you
And in your heart she will stay for ever through and through
We know you won't forget her or even let her go
But try to think of heaven and this you then must know
That Kylie is now happy in peace and so at rest
And you will not forget her 'cause to you she was the best

Deborah Elizabeth Gorman

MILESTONES OF SEPARATION

Milestones of separation, events through time,
Life blooming within my womb, made you mine,
A fruitful seed planted, a union that made me two,
The cord was cut, first separation for me and you.

Nurturing you at my breast, safe warm protected,
Devotion never wavered to keep you from life's harms.
Strong you grew, a happy child, dimples when you laughed,
First faltering steps another separation, you from my loving arms.

Another milestone quickly came your first day at school,
How big you looked, shiny shoes, rosy cheeks, school bag on
your back.
Flushed with excitement adventures ahead, friendships to be forged,
One more separation you turned, you smiled, you waved, I cried.

Adolescence came with all its woes, we had our ups and downs,
Muscles flexing but alas, too young to be the adult, too old to be
the child,
Tempers frayed, battles fought, sulking days, nights of worried
frowns,
Separation came again, where was the son that was once so mild?

A man you've grown, strong and true, my heart swells with pride,
In a uniform smart and blue, I see a handsome officer, a gentleman.
On life's oceans may you find a fair wind and calm seas,
We are separated by distance but anchored by chains of love.

Separations may take many forms, in journeys throughout life,
Filled with tears, reluctant steps, a lost lover or forbidden fruits,
Barbed words from jealous tongues, stubborn souls live in strife,
But nothing can separate a mother's memories, treasures locked safely
in your heart.

Helen Posgate

THE COAST ROAD

I followed coastal waters.
Twisting and turning
Through rustic harbours
Their names remembered
From childhood days
Spent fishing.

Bamburgh, sea houses, Amble,
Craster kippers for tea.
Arcades while away the hours,
Days of innocence,
'Only 10p more dad, please,'
So the children say.

Eating crab, dressed
For dinner what else,
And fizzy pop, what more,
Ice-cream and crazy golf.
The tide is turning
My life turns too.

Now, parent proud
Ten pence I gladly give
For a smiling face
And cast a line
In hope of catching
A childhood memory.

Colin Taylor

WHO OR WHOM

The girl stood, why was he late?
Her mind went numb, her body cold
Is this the man to love or hate?
Would others stay, his hand to hold?

She looked each way, please come, she prayed
My mind is numb, I love you so
My body's cold, but could be warm, yet I'm a afraid
No other one has treated me so

She looked again, the place was bare
Her face, her eyes showed how she cared
The man she loved, did he not care
To him, in everything, her soul had bared

She heard a noise, it must be him
Another man would make life grim
She shivered, could not move her head
O please be him, my heart, my body for you to wed

Standing in a corner dark
The only thought, to leave his mark
With movement slow their eyes then met
She knew his thoughts, her eyes were wet

Geof Farrar

ITALIAN REINCARNATION - 1953

Oh, I was home again -
Back where I knew that I belonged 'though
Parted by unnumbered floating years,
Now brought together and, at last, at peace.

This was not a place I'd been before
But, ah, the feel and taste and sense were known -
A memory of things past brought back to life.
I understood the language of this land
But could not speak it, and
These strangers were, I knew, my friends
Not just from this life but one long ago.
Chord upon chord struck memory's golden strand, and
There was no thing foreign in this foreign land.

Who had I been across the centuries?
What turn of fate had placed me there - and when?
I know not, but, then as now, I know I knew
Soft words, soft looks, music and laughter.
Shall I at any time be so beloved in the hereafter?

Patricia Bardell

THE GARDENS OF THE ROSES

Sad of heart and feeling low,
I reluctantly took a day out,
Went to St Alban's Rose Gardens.
Unknowing, what it, was about
Slowly emerging, through the gate
A fragrance - tickled my nose!
Lifting my eyes, to find the cause
I saw - the Gardens of the Rose!
If there is a heaven - this was it!
An amazing sight, all around
Roses, in every colour or kind
Spread over that hallowed ground.
Intoxicated with heavenly scent,
The perfection of every bloom.
I wandered around in a trance!
Gone - all trace of my erstwhile- gloom!
Senses reeling, in total delight,
Insignificant - every day woes
Disappeared - with nature personified,
In the Gardens of the Rose!

Evelyn Mary Eagle

MOUNTAIN SPLENDOUR

I will always remember,
My first trip
Up a Swiss mountain.
It was misty as we
Set off in the cable car.

As we went up higher
And could no longer
See the ground,
I felt as if I was
Leaving the world behind.

On nearing the top,
The sun came out
And turned the mountain
Into a beautiful picture,
I stepped out onto the snow.

It was like being
On top of the world,
Looking out onto the clouds
That seemed as if you
Could walk on them.

Standing in the snow
On the mountain top
The sun blazing down.
It was a magical day
I will never forget.

J M Judd

UNEXPECTED ENCOUNTER

You came in unexpectedly -
cosmeticised, of course, your hair
as brown as mine was grey; your skin
concealed by make-up skilfully
applied; a scarlet scarf your oriflamme -
imposing red on cream.

You came in unexpectedly -
as beautiful as when, some five
and twenty years before, I failed
to measure up to your idea of
what a future husband had to be.
And instantly the time gap closed:
two highlights of the past
recurred - that evening at the opera
(how innocent our London weekend was!)
- those moments in the afterglow
at Sandown Bay.

You came in unexpectedly and
brought a strange tranquillity -
my unexcited pulse maintained
its normal beat, unmoved by our
brief touch of hands - and yet I
felt a subtle change - contentment
with a rapport re-established.

I left soon afterwards, and when
alone, while whistling a pensive waltz
in keeping with the mood provoked,
I wondered if your feelings were
to be compared with mine.

Not that it really mattered . . . !

T C Hudson

THE SUMMER WASH

It turned cold suddenly and early
this year, it seemed to me.
Summer ended on Friday 11th September
to be precise.
Now wistfulness engulfs
at the dying of the light
   chilly rooms
      torpor
and the thought of donning
ever more layers of apparel until . . .
perhaps early May.

Yes, I know autumn is a bewitching time
for poets: so much mellowness,
russets, olives and ochres, bountiful
apple trees, crackling log fires, inglenooks,
and allusions to the dappled-ripeness
of one's year. Halcyon days.

But I ache for the summer wash: cadmiums,
scarlets and aquamarine; the voluptuous
waft of a giddy ocean breeze
over a grateful body,
lingering Andalusian nights
that melt into ardent, palmy days
when the indolent sun,
high and mighty, lolls resplendent
as it ordains the earth with lustre
and manifests the full-bloom of life.

Susan Serrano

KIRSTY

She came to us one February morn
6.50 am is when she was born
I looked at Anne, she looked at me
And spoke one word, Kirsty.

We gaze upon our little girl
Her head covered in a mass of curl
With eyes so wide she stares back at us
Probably wondering, what's all the fuss.

The years have passed she's fifteen now
Sometimes she's a little cow
She treats us as her personal slaves
And all she does is misbehaves.

Although she drives us really mad
We know she's really not that bad
We wouldn't want her not to be
We love our little Kirsty.

K J Wood

MEMORY LANE

Tiny legs skipped fast alongside you
One hand gripping a dripping ice
The other clutching your hand too
Bare feet treading on shaded flags
The bright ones burned - my shoes back at the 'digs'.

Past South Station where we just arrived the day before
Past the 'pub' with the big brown door
Then the shops with all good things galore
Buy me this, buy me that, buy me all the store.

On towards the sea, towards the sand
Still I clutched your gentle hand
Then I felt your hand grow tight
As I pulled towards the beach, which came in sight
As I hooted with joy, you let me go
Into the sand, into the yellow snow.

Now I walk the road again
Now fully grown, now feeling pain
Missing the firmness of your guiding hand
Now it's not the same, Dad,
Now it's not so grand.

Christopher J Whelan

OUR ANNIVERSARY

This is our first anniversary
And I still love you deeply
All the love that has been found
Together we are truly bound

People said we wouldn't make it
I didn't believe them one bit
We're not together always
Sometimes hours, sometimes days
But that's the way it had to go
Or it would be us no more

I've followed my heart to ends of the Earth
Wherever it may have led I've always found a way
To me a love so well worth
I just wish we could be together all day, every day

You and your beautiful face
Can never be replaced
One thing will always be true
I'll never stop loving you

This I promise you blue eyes
When I see you again
I'll try to give you happiness
And never cause you pain

With you I still feel great
Time for us to celebrate
Here's to the start of another year
With fun, love and passion with you my dear.

Donna Crocker

FAMILY WEDDING
(12th April 1997)

Today is the day you became man and wife
This is the first day of the rest of your life
Nobody knows what the future will hold
Stay close together, step out and be bold.

There'll be days you'll be happy
And days you'll feel sad
But even the worst days will not seem too bad
If you trust one another and show that you care
Be there for each other and everything share.

May God in his goodness surround you with love
Keeping watch o'er you both from his throne up above
Trust him at all times in all that you do
You'll have peace and contentment your whole life thro'

C Mackiggan

Our Gracious Queen Mother

You've come through those 'nervous nineties'
    And scored a century not out!
Today we salute you, a gracious lady,
    Who has served your people well without a doubt.

Having hesitated for good reason,
    You married Bertie, Duke of York;
You bore two beautiful princesses;
    And then began your noble work.

As George VI he acceded to the throne
    And you as Queen encouraged him each day.
He was surprised to find himself our king,
    But you stood by him, advising him and would pray.

In those terrible war years you showed compassion,
    Visiting those whose homes were reduced to cinders;
Then when your own home, too, was bombed you said:
    'I'm glad. Now we can face London's Eastenders.'

Today we see you stand in deep respect
    For millions slain in two world wars.
You support charities and cherish your family,
    Where'er you walk, we'll follow you with our prayers.

Though I have never met you close to hand,
    I feel, with many others, that I know you.
From you a radiance shines forth which comes from faith;
    It makes me long my deep gratitude to show you.

Lover of horses, ballet and us common folk,
    You identify with people everywhere.
Congratulations on your long and caring life,
    And may we all your peace and purpose share.

Robert Archer

LOVE STORY

Our first meeting was not exactly success personified
For I remember you and your friends teasing me 'til I cried
My 'pigtails' you tied around a lamp post
Then went off with your pals to have a good boast.
Your Big Brother found me and set me free
So that I could go home and have some tea.
From the age of eight 'til almost our teens
Our parents kept the peace 'tween us by any means.
Then came the gap of almost three years
Before we met up again without any fears.
My 'pigtails' were gone - in their place a 'ponytail'
And a figure which, for turning heads would never fail.
For your head turned - and mine did as well
As you were an 'Adonis'; and in love we fell.
That years holiday was the best of my life
And if I hadn't been stupid I could have been your wife.
Oh we were in love - there was no one else around
Caresses and kisses for weeks did abound.
When I had to go home, oh, how I cry
And your eyes too, were not exactly dry.
We vowed our love then and forevermore
Our parting that day really cut to the core.
As the years passed I was stupid enough to roam
Which would not have happened if we'd had a phone.
In those days they were few and far between
Not exactly part of our household scene.
Throughout my life I've regretted making you sad,
Many times that thought has almost made me go mad.
I've always loved you, this I know now for sure
As in your arms I have always felt loved and secure.

Failed marriages and wasted years, are now behind me,
And the trip I made to meet you, made me clearly see
That my future happiness lies now within your power
Tell me please, can our love come again into flower?
If the answers no, this I'll quite understand
But if yes, then I'll be the happiest in the land.

Margaret Phillips

THE WARMTH OF SUNSHINE

I have fallen, willingly into your embrace.
Yet, I can't imagine what made me trip, or slip or fall.
If I were someone else, something else, then maybe.
Yet you have brought the warmth of sunshine to my face
and now I can wade in the radiance of contentment.

I think I have felt this luminescence before,
within the delicate dances of trees,
their out-stretched arms, beckoning.
The sensuous rhythms of the depthless shores, inviting.
A kiss from the breeze, a laugh never heard before, until now.

Yet you, you regenerate the warmth of sunshine
and I feel honoured that you chose to shine on me.
I feel precious, sacred, pure,
enlightened, rekindled.
Yet most of all,
I feel,
I feel free.

Louise Grace Ward

RETIREMENT ANY TIME

I love to sit, ponder over breakfast,
To think whilst devouring juice, cereal, toast and tea,
What is happening today? What will happen today?
Wonderful new thoughts and ideas are really up to me,
Must move, look, feel, smell and see!
Beyond the door the air and beautiful scenery are free!

Joan Marsh

A WALK BY THE SEA

As I walked by the sea one day,
A lady touched my arm to say;
God is with you, He'll help you dear,
To have Him with you, there's nothing to fear.

Now how did she know how I was feeling,
That very moment my mind was reeling;
God must have sent her with those kind words,
To give me hope and relieve my fears.

Kindness and love ends all your troubles,
Knowing God's with you, your strength will be doubled;
He'll give you help in times of need,
Just ask the Lord your soul to feed.

You'll find in the end you will be a winner,
So pray to the Lord, you will be a singer;
Wake up each day and sing His songs,
For with God on your side you can't go wrong.

Thelma Cook

SEEING STARS

Last night I saw a shooting star,
It flew o'erhead to where you are.
I know I was supposed to wish,
For some extraordinary treat,
But all I've ever wished for is,
To see you and to hold you close.
And in that split second in time,
As it flew high above my head,
I thought of you -
And how my wish remains undone.
Because to me you cannot come.
Cross my heart and hope to die,
One day I'll reach my heart's desire.

Andy Bryan

THE AVENUE

As I walk down the avenue
narrow cobbled road no grassy view
back to back house, small and bleak,
rented, in poor repair, our health defeats.

Wooden lathe, plaster and hair walls
riddled with vermin bug ridden as a result.
This was home for eleven years
caused sickness in children misery and tears.

Diphtheria, whooping cough, bronchitis severe,
coal fired, smog atmospheres, could not be cleared.
All added to the fight to keep clean,
contributing to the post-war misery.

Outside privy copper with stack
was lit for hot water, the grime to attack.
Clothes washed by hand, bath once a week,
our mothers struggled, illness to defeat.

Memories of the fear I felt at night
crossing the yard to the privy without light.
When winter came and the water pipes froze,
cold seemed to freeze my very bones.

Children who survived those severe years
appreciate our mothers' loving care,
without their fighting tenacity
a barren land, this would have been.

The toll in stress and health was great
alone the mothers in this war waged
honoured by none, but we who remember
whose survival was mothers only agenda.

Evelyn Poppy Sawyer

WHEN GRAN WAS SMALL

We sat around our fireplace,
Contentment shone from ev'ry face,
My parents, Patrick, me and John.
Then Daddy put the kettle on.
'Now Ann,' he said, 'let's make some tea;
It's very easy, just watch me!'
But barges hooted on the river
So dolefully they made me shiver.

Then cosy warmth enfolded me
And flick'ring shadows danced with glee.
Mum's copperware gleamed fiery red
While molten gold o'er mirrors spread
Until they glistened with delight.
But I clutched Teddy very tight
For barges called me from the river
So hauntingly they made me shiver.

Asthmatic gas lights wheezing and breathed
And bursting chestnuts sputt'ring seethed.
The cherry firewood crackled spit,
Spry schools of sparks the chimney lit.
Then Mummy prayed by candlelight
And kissed us all and said goodnight.
Those barges must have slept, I'm sure,
For in my bed I heard no more.

But now I'm old and reminisce,
I'd love to hear those hot logs hiss.
Then by the fire our knees we'd roast
And gladly eat Mum's dripping toast.
At jacks upon the rug we'd play
And be together ev'ry day.
Those barges weird have lost their dread,
But Mom and Dad have gone ahead.

Beryl-Ann Böhringer

THE WAHINE

Wet to waist the wahine
Waddled up the beach
Left the lonely fishing boat
Dragged out of the sea

Hair black to the waist
Adorned with flowers so fresh
Plump and plain the face
Baked and brown the skin

Simple white the blouse
A floral skirt clung wet
Fleshy fish her catch
Quivering hung from waist

Greetings as she passed
In a strange and southern tongue
A figure seen of this land
Where her proud life began.

George Carle

FEEDING THE DRAGON

Good times clinging to the rail
heading for the skies, like
a dragon's tail;
Sun on the face, a joy to share
with nations of the world
in a cable car;
Laughter has a language
of its own - second
to none;
A sense of integration,
only halfway
to heaven;
Suddenly, journey ends,
world rushes in through
camera lens,
marking out the same
old boundaries
again;
Scales of a dragon
misting over
the sun

R N Taber

SPECIAL TIMES

Shall I take a trip down memory lane
I'll take it with you in mind
That night I sat upon your knee
And we had a good old kissing time
Those times were special
For you were the romantic kind
That amethyst gem you placed
Around my neck
Created a moment for all the rest
They admired it with words of the best
Their pealing voices splendoured on
That's nice, that's beautiful, that's pretty.
Are now stored away in my memory chess.

Carolie Pemberton

ON BECOMING A GRANDMOTHER

When I first heard the news on the day of your birth,
The world was more beautiful with you here on earth.
You're coming to us, meant one thing to me,
It brought me nearer to my immortality.

Whatever may be dealt you in the game of life we play,
These blessings I would hope for, and pray for you each day.
For you, health in abundance, for no money can this buy.
Humour, for often in this world there is much to make us cry.

Should you be blessed with talents, whatever they may be,
Let no arrogance, or pride be yours, just humility.
That God may be beside you in your life, that come what may,
He will always love and guide you, every step along your way.

Jill M Kimber

I REMEMBER TO THIS VERY DAY

I remember well to this very day, a time spent in open fields -
a mother's hand to guide me through that Promised Land.
It was a day, I believe, blessed indeed by heaven's ways -
smells divine, coming from flowers wild, sounds of birds
from overhead, searching eyes looked for clouds in vain.
I had the beauty of nature's ways, the love of a mother true -
thoughts that will stay with me, until I have to make my leave.

Rowland Patrick Scannell

BELVEDERE REVISITED

Five years down the road
And still in your company.
Held in my memory
The magic which you wove.

The seating's rearranged
But hearts still in their place.
Whilst greeting me each cheery face
Has nothing more to prove.

The spell of Paleokastritsa
Lingers on.
Its welcome surely has not gone.
Shining through the eyes of love.

I breathe the sweet air slowly
As summers pass me by.
I feel the need to cry
But I'm afraid to move.

Another year is ending fast;
So many changes on the way.
So few days left for me to say,
'My thanks for all the care you gave.'

Tina Watkin

THE SIXTIES

Welcome to the sixties I've been waiting here for you
Sitting quietly thinking as the sixties often do
Life is getting older, it's building up a past
Enjoying all there is to do and trying to make it last

There are memories there to treasure, there is doing all you can
There's lots of life for living, there's the future still to plan
And as you leave the fifties there's not a lot that's new
Perhaps you do it slower and some times not on cue

Welcome to the sixties it's great to come that far
And better still when you stop to think what the other options are
Time is but a highway that we travel in our life
With those we love to share it, family, friends and wife

Though youth is long since over, may it live on in your mind
May your sixties prove as happy yet as the decades left behind
If life starts getting slower don't bridle at the pace
Life is there for living it's not a constant race

Ray Ryan

THE ONE I LOVE

Stop the sun, hold back the day,
For the one I love is far away.
So on the day we had to part,
With her kiss I packed my heart.
There's no more laughter, no more smiles,
For between us lie so many miles.
At night I wake and call her name,
But the answer always stays the same.
This quiet house, my lonely tear,
Again I clutch her picture near.
And to my body tightly press,
To make the loneliness a little less.
I count the days till she returns,
When again my world will start to yearn.
For the day again when she is here,
And I kiss her face and hold her near.

For this loneliness cuts like a knife,
Because my darling you are

My love!
My life!

C D G

FINEST HOUR

Looking back upon my life
my finest hour I can recall,
was the birth of my daughter Erin,
she was really cute and small.

Holding her for the first time on
the second of February nineteen ninety-two,
was a feeling I will never forget,
holding a life, a life that was new.

Precious little bundle
that was born into this world,
she is my lovely daughter,
the finest hour, my baby girl.

N McManus

SPORTS DAY

I wasn't there to win
I was there to do my best
I was there to show I was willing to compete
Stand proud with my pigeon chest
It was the school sports day
I ran the sprint with no delay
There was no action replay
Cheats appeared on that 2nd of May
I was awarded fourth place
Though I knew I'd came in second
Being robbed was not to my taste
I argued until I was blue in the face
A teacher intervened saying he'd seen the race
I was not to be disgraced
I took my rightful place
Standing with smiling face
My silver medal I embraced

John Beals

DOWN THE AISLE

A shaft of bright light fell
On her snow-white wedding dress
As she slowly walked down the aisle
And thousands of sunbeams from her veil
Dancing around her beautiful face.

I gazed upon the pew, where the guests
Were all smiles
Fluttered at the bride my tiny handkerchief,
Then I turned around hastily
To dab the warm tears of joy and pride.
Thrilled, I watched my destiny's hand
Rebuild the far, far away past
Into the shape of new events to come,
And all the unforeseen moments,
That accompany them so fast.

It seemed like yesterday,
But is also seemed like a long time ago,
When she was just born,
Between happiness and emptiness
I felt cheerful, I felt tearful,
Oh . . . almost torn.

'All the best Mrs Morrison!'
I whispered and sighed
As my girl withstood my searching eyes,
With her pretty head tilted to one side,
She looked like a sunflower
In the warmth of sunrise.

Like diamond drops of water
Catching the silverish light,
Her eyes quickly met the wonder,
In my eyes,
Then in the raining confetti
She smiled beautifully,
As if to say
This doesn't really mean goodbye.

Jane Soroush

COUNSELLING COURSE

Not knowing quite what to expect, we came along nervous and taxed
With tutor's cheerful countenance, soon we were chatting and relaxed

To stop the class from wasting time once social chit-chat had begun
She would say in her unique way 'Everyone - listen - everyone!'

When we voted for coffee break she'd get up for to quench our thirst
Mind you it would have been more use if she'd put the plug switch
                                                                down first

No umbrage taken, we just laughed when she kept muddling up
                                                          our names
Thinking it of little import; we were striving for higher aims

In *role-play* we all practised to gain prowess in confrontations
We're now able to cope *so* well with aggressive situations

She pulled us out of ignorance, assisting us in clarity
Doing it all with such aplomb, congruence and sincerity

Informing us of gen to ken were sheets of quarto week by week
Giving us all that was needed to unfurl counselling mystique

With newly acquired confidence, there's no telling how far we'll go
For each and everyone of us can deal with all scenario

Such tolerance and empathy plus genius in basic skills
Cannot fail to impress the world by solving every client's ills

Course will be missed - it is the end; strict routine changed our
                                                          lazy ways
No need to get up so early: *what will we do on Saturdays?*

Tina Lipman

FRIENDS

You've all helped me through such strife
Been there in all the bad times in my life
And the only thing that pulled me through
Was knowing I had a true friend in you.

Tina, you gave me good advice
To me you've always been very nice
I hope I can help you in the same way
If you ever need me one day.

Lyndsay, my Seth, you are so kind
You put a smile on my face, make me feel fine
You put up with me playing boring games
Only a true friend would have the patience.

Gemma, the bestest friend I've ever known
We've laughed, we've cried, we've had fights with bath foam
I really do hope that we all stay in touch
Because I will miss you all so very much.

Jodie McKane

WHERE IS IT?

Whatever happened to it?
It was there when I last looked.
I remember admiring it
As my skirt I hooked.
Good heavens - this
Is not to my taste,
Whatever happened
To my waist?

T Kellgren

REMEMBERING

The musty smell of old, damp hay
Takes me back to childhood years.
'Come Nick, come Nobbin - step this way!'
Old Tom would say, leading the shires
Up to the top field, past where we'd play,
Encamped within the ruined byre.

And apple blossom's sweet bouquet,
Redolent upon the breeze!
Smell it now, and it's yestermay -
That orchard with its old, gnarled trees:
Tramping through it on our way
To net tadpole and water fleas.

Later, when the orchards fruited,
We turned outlaw, truth to tell.
Like all the other kids, 82
we looted:
Apples, pears and plums as well;
Gorged ourselves till satiated.
(If spotted, we could run like hell!)

Remember, up in Clay Lane woods,
Trees festooned with fat cob nuts?
Never seem to taste that good
These days - is that just growing up?
But then, I guess that nothing could
Compare with memory's brimming cup.

Colin Wright

FOUR-LEAFED CLOVER

I will lie beside you
   So you and I may lie
And count the stars that glow
   And view the endless sky
And feel the cool green grass
   And hear the whispering wind
And watch the clouds that pass
   And see if we can find
Ourselves a four-leaf clover
   And if you hold my hand
We need not search forever
   So come and lie with me
And when I feel you near
   I know that I will see
My very precious four-leaf clover.

Joan Elizabeth Blissett

THE GOOD OLD DAYS

Waking up frozen in icy-cold air,
Frost on the windows and linoed floor bare,
No central heating - warm carpets were rare,
Good old days? Yes, I remember them well!

Crossing the yard to the wooden shack loo,
Pants down round ankles and all your parts blue,
No warm inside toilet - (you haven't a clue),
Good old days? Yes, I remember them well!

Breaking the ice on the rainwater tub,
Carbolic soap helped you have a good scrub,
No hot water taps then, or hot showers before grub,
Good old days? Yes, I remember them well!

Cooking with fire on black-leaded range
That wouldn't get hot whate'er you arrange,
No gas or electric, no microwave strange,
Good old days? Yes, I remember them well!

Bath-times were Saturdays, zinc tub off the wall,
Heating up water, enough for us all,
Taking our turns, we'd have *such* a ball,
Good old days? Yes, I remember them well!

Washday was Monday, with clothes wet and mangled,
Scrubbing and 'poshing' and pegged out and dangled,
No washing machines or spin-dryers new-fangled,
Good old days? Yes, I remember them well!

The roads were quite safe for kids out to play,
One car an hour was the norm for the day,
No radios or TVs, no computers to play,
Good old days? Yes, I remember them well!

G K (Bill) Baker

A SPECIAL DAY

Dear sister, the baby of us all
who I've watched through time grow up in times of stress
we all share of us we our parents have lost.

Your sister-in-law and I are pleased
Dear sister of mine with cheerful face you have always
had, we act as parents
on your wedding day with honour and love in my heart.

Are pleased to give you away
on this your wedding day baby sister of mine.
Your big brother of three this of
that I am.

With brothers, sons, nephews and nieces
may this be the best day of all
in your life and give happiness to you
through time in your life.

This, that you deserve free from stress
in your life you have encountered for one so young the baby
sister of us all who I've watched
in life grow up.

This from the heart, from your oldest brother
of all who have seen three grow up when you of your
days were born into this world had come.
A special time for you baby sister of mine
another step for you in life to tread.

A special time in this year 2000 September 16.
A happy wedding day dear sister of
three brothers of yours
on your wedding day.

Arthur May

To My Daughter On Her Wedding Day

The day that you were born
Was snowy, clear and bright,
I was the proudest mum in all the world.

Through all your growing years,
Though we had many a fight,
I was the proudest mum in all the world.

You rode, you swam, you danced,
For you it all came right,
I was the proudest mum in all the world.

You chose to be a nurse
And showed your shining light,
I was the proudest mum in all the world.

Now standing at the altar
Alongside your Mr Right
I am the proudest mum in all the world
Forgive me if I cry!

Joan Gray

THOUGHTS OF A PREGNANT WOMAN

All the joys and dreams reverberating the sun
Hang upon me like a precious crown,
The barriers to God's spirit are being broken
So that his will may be done on earth.
Time and eternity are taking flesh in me.

Take my body, take my blood,
Multiply your cell, find all the space
To grow and know your mother.
I drink milk, I eat good food,
I take rests between chores to love you into life.
You float free from gravity
In my amniotic sea.
Your form, your face,
Synthesis in a newness
Of all who went before,
Envisioning those who will follow.

My child, the moment of your inception
Is a breakthrough, a divine explosion
Transforming me into a holy vessel.
My little one, you already give me signs
Of the life to come.
When you are ready
Push open my narrow gate
And, free, bear the weight of air.
I will suckle you at my breast,
Guard your growth and raise you.
You, silence-word-act,
Pregnant in my heart,
Will never depart from me.

Angela C M

MY THREE GRANDSONS

Joshua was our first grandchild
who was in a hurry to be born,
for he arrived five weeks early
on an early July morn.
He came just in time for his
grandad to hold and love,
for just two months later
Grandad Reg went to heaven above.
Harrison was my next grandson
a miracle I believe,
he was an unexpected baby
born on Christmas Eve.
Two weeks later Thomas arrived
eight days into this millennium,
I look at the wonder of all three
and I cherish my life with them throughout
the years to come.

Yvonne Lewis

MY PROMISE

My wedding is just a memory
That I'll remember until I die
It really meant so much to me
And it still makes me sigh
I held onto my father's arm
As he walked me down the aisle
I wasn't feeling very calm
When you met me with a smile
I vowed that I would love you
Until the end of life
Then you became my husband
And I became your wife
Now many years have gone by
And we are still together
And just like my promise
I'll be loving you forever.

Marie Horridge

MY FRIEND

A man that walks the hills
He is, as tall as the sky
At peace with the world
The beauty he sees
He keeps in his heart.
A smile on his face
The wind in his hair
The deer and the eagle
Are his company.

Carole A Cleverdon

GIVE ME A BABY

Give me a baby, make my life complete
This unbeating passion, I know you can't beat
I have it all, but yet I have none
The only thing I yearn is a son
Two daughters and a puppy too
Is it too much to ask just a small thing to do
Why can't God bless us two
Me and my two daughters, with eyes so blue
I brought a puppy so big and bold
A little something for me to hold
But yet I cry and cry in vain
For a son, to give him your name
Why do I feel so bad
All I want is a strapping lad
To need, to love and to hold, to keep
A child of mine, for this I weep
I love Nigel, Katie and Becky too
And Charlie the dog for all I do
But I have room for one more
A little gem, not a daily chore
My unborn child for this I pine
Please God above, make it mine

Tracey Marie

WAITING TIME

Behind my quiet, lonely smile
Behind my silent tear
My thoughts are once again of you
And wish that you were here
I see your smile, your patient smile
Your look of love so dear
As long ago, so long ago
Your arms they held me near
I try to hide my loneliness
Tho folk so kind can be
So that my 'missing you' won't show
My tears they will not see
As days and nights go slowly by
This world turns once again
My eyes they cry
They will not dry
Till we are one again.

Joan Winwood

GLENCOE

He was a Queen Scout
His was the camping gear
And I set out alone
to the Outer Hebrides.

Easy journey to Scotland
hitch-hiking
But at the border grew harder
Hours spent at the side of the road.
But something nearly always stopped
from 10 tonner to bubble car.
Stayed with elderly relatives to Airdrie
slipped back on the morning road again.

Evening streets of Glencoe
full up youth hostel
standing on village street with two Americans
sun going down over the mountains
mountain reflected in the large sea lochs
reflecting the red and the golden sky
and beyond, more misty mountains
extending as far as the eye can see.

Philip Loudon

HOLIDAYS

In a mist in a daze,
The way you act does amaze,
Summer's joy, autumn's haze,
Youth's energetic ways,
Reminis your holidays,
Think of me always,
The ocean has refreshing sprays,
On the beach relax and laze,
Imagination always strays,
When sitting under the sun's rays,
Upon fish the seagull prays,
Bank holiday traffic delays,
The sea has a shiny summer glaze,
Upon the beach a child plays,
The light hearted approach always pays,
Though always wanting longer stays.

Sarah Morgan

RETRIBUTION

The world in which we live in has gone beyond control,
Millions are starving and death exacts its toll.
There's food enough for everyone, but due to selfish greed,
The powers that be refuse to share the food that people need.
They monopolise the markets that sell grain for bread,
Result, millions of people live in misery and dread.
They can't afford the prices that are so sky high,
They fight a losing battle and millions of them die.
What an indictment, its plain for all to see,
The money barons of the world creating poverty.
They plough their ill-gotten seeds of wealth,
Into weapons of carnage and war, in just a human lifetime.
Their hands are blood soaked claws
That sacrificed the flower of youth on the altar of selfish gain.
There's epitaphs around the world of the millions that were slain,
They gather round their cenotaphs erected with great pride,
Anyone can go and read the names of those who died,
There is no sanctity of life in the world today,
It's just a human jungle, where the poor become the prey,
Of greedy avaricious men who deals in stocks and shares,
And poor innocent people, become the victims of their snares.
But justice will be metered out the bible tells us so,
The sands of time are running out, all wickedness must go,
The earth will yield its increase, for all the world to share,
The bounty of God's goodness and of his loving care,
The earth restored to paradise, a glorious sight to see,
The beauty of creation and true *theocracy*.

E G Werrett

SUMMER WEDDING

The Admiral and the painted lady
dressed in their best finery - were married
just has dawn was breaking
over the forest canopy
Sweet dawn chorus heralded a new day
ragged robin - marsh marigold - flag iris
stood has attendants
Whortberry - hawthorn - bramble
stood in guard of honour
The meadow queen afficiated
honoured invited guests included
Dragon and demoiselle fly - ladybird too
lady fern, ladies smock to name just a few
Brimstone, wall, peacock, hovered nearby
Woodland hare bells and bluebells
ring out their happy tune to send them on their way
as they flew away together on that
summer morning breeze.

David Charles

THE ELLESMERE BOWL

That old craftsman worked with care,
He knew its worth,
That last dab of lustre on the earthenware.
He made the bowl, the foot he fettled,
The pattern he indented
And after that, another theme he settled
Old nature re-invented.
The tendrils flowed, plants take up their stations
And scarlet flowers spread their petals wide,
Throwing green from side to side.
Then across the indentations
Fell from loaded brush, the rich cobalt.
On that a glint of almost secret lustre
His seeming vague enrichment's rich result.

And now I see he knew what he was doing
Now in gloaming dusk, new light is brewing
A steady gleam as from a garnet crystal
                          pours from the rim
Far down the room a light that's dim
Returns with lustrous blaze
No twinkling star but steady through the haze
All from this earthen pot
This ceramic grounding, pre-porcelain child of the Earth,
                          of granite rot.

For, as the pot, we have no other heritage for leaven,
No other capital, earth is our only ancestry.
But this one source is given.
All there, for all, and most of all in primativity
We have no rights
We are not free

There is responsibility
Our capital, our Earth, our universe for us to use
                    - remember - it is interest free.
This potter used two pounds of it
To make a basin with a garnet light
                    illuminating me.

Catherine Moody

My Dream

My dream was to sleep out on the high fells
And rise to the call of the skylark so
The sun raising its head above fell tops
Would dab each and every peak with a golden glow
As I wandered the fells peace was reigning
This world had dissolved all the sound
A pale grey mist kept its distance
But accompanied me on my way as I roamed round
Occasionally the grey veil was lifted
As the sun tried to pierce the pale mist
A red deer crossed the line of my vision
As I wondered what other views I had missed
I wanted to stay in this land forever
In this land of peace without end
But the pale grey mist was dissolving
So once more to the lowlands I had to descend
For this moment my dream may be over
But I know I can always return so
My dream to sleep out on the high fells
And to watch the sun rise with its golden glow.

F J Dunn

FIRST IMPRESSIONS

Here he is
We've waited months
Nine months
A fragile baby boy
My boy
Our boy
Ten little toes
Ten little fingers
I'm excited and calm all at the same time
Nurse
Is his head all right?
It seems to be swollen
Yes, yes that's normal
My wife is absolutely knackered
Well of course
I hold my son
Wrapped in his little sheet
I look deeply
Lovingly
Into his eyes
I quietly talk
I can't stop talking
Letting him know
I am here
His father
Wow!
He's fantastic
Here he is
We've waited months
Nine months

Colin Farquhar

VICTORY AT THE OVAL, 2000

'Twas years ago in sixty-nine,
When England won and that was fine;
Throughout the intervening years,
We've lost and suffered many fears.

The Oval Test was real top rate,
The batting, bowling, fielding great!
Atherton strove to stay at crease,
His century, a feat that brought new lease.

Ambrose and Walsh, real world stars,
Their farewell honoured from near and far;
Their exploits together, for year on year,
Brought honours and glory, caused much fear.

For Gough and Caddick, the series was great,
Both White and Cork were often first rate;
Trescothick truly gained his place,
His stand with Atherton provided the base.

To Captain and Coach we sing our praise,
Together their work our spirits doth raise;
With Pakistan, Australian matches to come,
There is surely hope, we might beat the drum.

John Paulley

AGAIN

At ten years old, I was quick and bold,
And my days were filled with joy,
I had a wealth of strength and health,
I was such a happy boy,
Every single day I was out to play,
It was always warm and bright,
I would spend the time with a friend of mine,
And a catapult or kite,
Or we'd fish and dream at a nearby stream,
Though we never saw a scale,
And I used to wish I could catch a fish,
With proportions like a whale,
Other boys would shout, let us see your trout,
Or some other cheeky crack,
Then I'd lie and say I caught ten today,
But I always put them back,
I felt such a fool on some days at school,
When we had to dance with girls,
Coming face to face with that giggling race,
With their perfume and their curls,
Yet I've often dreamed of the day it seemed,
Like a bolt from up above,
Made my senses whirl when I saw the girl,
Who awakened me to love,
I've had some tears down through the years,
And an ample share of pain,
Yet still today I can truly say,
I would do it all again.

Matthew L Burns

FIRST CHILD

White faced balloon.

Nozzled to the quiet
Tug of milk
You half sleep;

One eye a sudden
Cracked egg, the other
Fixed in the albumen
Roll of orbit.

Already you are a
Tiny, jealous god,
A week's worth
Of breath conjuring

Squalls, the hot squawk
Of displeasure
Like raw, red meat.

In your lace jackboots
You demand
The propitiation
Of the creamy nub of stars

While our own lungs brim
That which
Is hallowed beyond all names.

Martyn Lowery

ONE LAST SIGN

The river flows and trickles,
A cloud passes by,
I feel your soft presence,
It will never die.
The sky is vast and open,
The air is fresh but warm,
The world passes by peacefully,
I know you've come to no harm.
I picture you as a young girl,
Clambering carefully across the rocks,
Holding up the hem of her dress,
Being careful with her best summer frock.
She carries a wicker basket,
With pebbles up to the brim,
She clasps one in her little hand,
Then over the water she watches it skim.
I know this is a special day,
A special moment for us to share,
I know this is our last goodbye,
A special message, oh so rare.
I finally can let you go,
I know that you're at peace,
I know one day I'll see you again,
For now I'll be at ease.
I sigh one last sigh for you,
I can't help one last tear,
It's a sign of acceptance,
Everything's perfectly clear.
The moment's nearly over now,
But I see one last sign,
A bird swoops gracefully through the sky
And that picture will always be mine.

Emma Wellington

THE BIRTH DAY

Lying on the trolley gazing at the cracks in the ceiling
Waiting . . . waiting . . .
It comes again - face distorted and a body wracked with pain
What is that screaming noise . . . can it be me?
Faces all above me - a dark dress with a silver buckle
Someone holds my hand and mops my brow
Mutter . . . mutter . . .
Not yet, not fully dilated. . . another half an hour . . .
Oh God! When will it be over, why am I left here alone?
Why isn't he here with me; why shouldn't he know what I am
Suffering?

Once again the pain, I grip the sides of the trolley and bite my tongue
I try not to scream again but I have no control
Suddenly I am being wheeled along
Then gently lifted onto a cool white sheet
Again that awful pain
Push . . . push . . .
We can see the head they say, just pant for now
Push . . . push . . .
Nearly there . . .
Push . . . push . . . one big push . . .
The head is free
Just one more push and
Slither . . . slither . ..
Well done!

I lay back on the pillows exhausted but elated
They clean me up and wipe the sweat from my body
I close my eyes
From across the corridor comes the sound of the radio
Jean Metcalfe and Cliff Michelmore presenting Family Favourites
On a Sunday lunchtime

Here you are Mother - I open my eyes
And they hand me a small cocoon of blanket
Showing a tiny, perfect face; it crumples up into a big yawn;
My God! It's like looking at him, how he will love her
But for now she is mine, totally and utterly mine
My beautiful little daughter
On her birth day

O V Hopson

ACROSS BRADFORD VIA PRAGUE

I had been scurrying through the streets of Bradford
Sweating uncomfortably in the humidity
As my tasks had multiplied
But the time for their completion had diminished
I grew enervated and irritable
As I descended Darley Street
Until an unbidden recollection crossed my mind
Of the steep descent from the castle in Prague
Where John and I had struggled to recall its history
Before seeking respite from our tourist exhaustion
We came down that famous hill
And discovered a labyrinthine ginnel
Which led to a terraced garden
And umbrella shaded tables
The smell of lavender vied with that of omelettes
The colours of potted summer flowers
Painted the afternoon with happy shades
While a jazz trio played subtle variations
On hummable melodies
And we sat and drank and chatted
For a most contented hour.

This memory could not ease the schedule I obeyed
As I accelerated into Hustlergate
Late for my next call
But it mellowed me and made me feel
An outward moving smile from heart and mind to lip;
And a joy at the thought of that time and that place
Shared in happy mood with one I loved.

Nicholas Howard

BAPTISM

Let lips of little children sing
Of Him this lifelong day.
Within whose arms, all glowing warm,
A tender baby lay.
All joyous be whom truly see
The peace wherein he lies.
Quiet as death, the fleeting breath,
Its riches realise.

And oh the bliss, the heavn'nly kiss,
Born of Thy kingdom now.
Without measure, Thy sure treasure
Is poured upon the brow.
So soft as dew, the brimming brew,
And pure as any wine.
The source of life, the strength in strife,
The graft upon the vine.

Aye verily, sing merrily,
In this baptismal hour.
Let none impart the faintest heart,
Nor aye eschew Thy pow'r.
And thine the right and thine the might,
Bestown for all to see.
This precious birth, mere Mother Earth
Hath nought compared to Thee.

Derek F Haskett-Jones

KIDS' STUFF

A long time ago when just a kid,
No limit to the things we did.
Running barefoot to the moat,
Picnics - jam butties and cake we'd tote.
A lemonade bottle, full of cold tea,
Hop, skip and jumping - laughing with glee.

Summers were long then, the sun always shone
And we were happy as the day was long.
A jam jar we'd take, with handle of string
To put our tiddlers and tadpoles in,
We'd caught with a net, trying hard not to pitch,
Head first into a green, slimy ditch.

'Stop getting under my feet!' Mum would say,
'Get your coats on and go out and play.'
Not needing much prodding, we're off like a shot -
With a warning from Mum, which we soon forgot.
'Don't go too far now, tea's ready at five,
Be back before Father, or he'll skin you alive.'

'Oh! No you don't, just come in here'
Mum's voice carried, angry, loud and clear.
'Now, that's enough, you heard what I said;
In here you lot - now get up to bed.
What have I told you, I'll teach you to fight.'
(There was no supper for us that night!)

Dad, crafty, kept out of her way,
He'd be off to his local, if he'd got his pay.
Memories of times, some sad, some sweet,
What we had then, none can repeat.
The legacies of childhood are flown all too fast,
So make the most of them - while they last.

Doris Farran

NEXT SUNDAY

I'm going to a christening -
I wonder who'll be there?
My cousin, Timothy, will be
Entrusted to God's care.
His candle will shine brightly,
To show what faith can do
In lightening life's darker times
For him - and me and you.
We'll be so very happy,
All admire him, one by one -
Then join a jolly party,
Play games and have such fun.

Beryl M Smith

TOPSY

A long time ago when I was three
A gift was given with love to me
Wrapped in brown paper tied with string
My excitement was high as I peeked in
What I saw was a doll inside
Which I cherished dearly and loved with pride
Made of rag in a green knitted suit
A pom-pom hat yet she wore no boots
Topsy her name I decided would be
That little doll went everywhere with me
Then one day off we went to the park as a special treat
A day I will never forget, I left Topsy behind on the seat
Back I was taken I looked in vain
I remember calling out her name
Yet never again was I to see
My playmate and friend, lovely Topsy.

Doreen Biddiscombe

NINETEEN

My son, today as you attain the age of nineteen years,
I wonder, with astonishment acute,
How come I never noticed when the Gerbers changed to beers;
The Johnsons into Aramis and Brut?

Now, placed and graded like a peach, all smiles and gleaming eyes
As you depart for university,
The world is yours; in three years you'll be infinitely wise . . .
(Or is it just a matter of degree?)

Sure it was only yesterday . . . but hindsight's view is blind.
You're adult-groomed and suitably careered.
So why do I keep seeing, in this vision of the mind,
That baby, capped and gowned, and with a beard?

Brenda Young

HE IS HERE

Here I lie in bed feeling sorry for myself,
Aching tummy, pounding head.
Days and nights seem the same,
It would be nice if someone came.
A cup of tea just made for me,
A cuddle to know someone cares for me.
This is the time when you're feeling low,
You really think you are on your own.
But through it all you realise,
That there is one who really cares.
Just turn to God and you will find,
He has been with you all the time.

Parris Perry

ON THE MORNING TIDE

9.30 at a Portsmouth dockside.
The clouds, the family crowds,
shed tears just a little, on this windy August morning.
Naval uniforms, cranes, buzzing planes.
A marine band and as the haunting music drifts over the grey waves,
there surely the spirits of Drake and Nelson,
smile down on such an English scene.
For the ships and the people may have changed,
but the emotions and loyalties that drove those men to sea,
remain the same.
A few remembered other homecomings.
Springtime exercises, Type 22 destroyers.
The Glamorgan, The Battle-Axe, The Sheffield.
For some did not have this happy outcome.
People wave and shout,
'Here she comes,'
The Illustrious grey and grave.
Eyes searching the decks, heart banging.
The gangways down so slowly.
The constricting throat that cannot say a word.
Arms open and enclose a forgotten warmth
that wraps you in intense, personal safety.
Cores of steel in our ships.
Cores of steel in our men.
The Senior Service, of whom we should be very proud,
are home again.

A' O' E'

CHANGES

The birth of my son changed my life
I became a mother not just a wife
It was a special time that day for me
It unlocked in my heart a significant key.

Change, change of a particular kind
It opened my heart, it blew my mind.
A little baby I had produced
An armistice, a kind of truce.

He brought together my husband and I
A son for him would satisfy.
I felt within that hour strong
I even felt the need for song.

It was the only time there was no war
For soon we were to be ignored.
My husband chose the pubs to us
We let him go without a fuss.

And life went on in the usual way
Never knowing from day to day.
Then one day he left and life did change
We had to think and rearrange.

My son and I did many things
He was too old for seesaws and swings.
No, off to the theatre and pictures too
Lots of things as he grew.

Now it's fishing all the time
He tells me how the rocks he climbs.
Another change, another way
That's the way it is today.

Denise Shaw

ON BECOMING A GODMOTHER

Yes decidedly all pink with a tiny turned up nose
The cutest little fingers and the sweetest little toes
All decked out in finery and trimmed with blue only the best
This was to be my Godchild and I must really take interest
I have to pick him up and hold him in a special way
He blinks and gurgles as he wriggles he's safe I sway
The rhythm is soothing and very soon he is asleep
Rehearsing for his christening my goodness does not come cheap

He is a loveable little mite so small and compact
His mother residing over all is delighted I never held back
To be a Godmother to their son I'd never been one before
Feeling this is an honour as my charge emits a roar
He requires a nappy change just as well mother is at hand
I view the strange procedure my Godson would not ban
He is perfection as he is made clean and tidy
Now he requires feeding I do those honours nicely

Bottle fed how convenient and he gulps away
He frequently has to be burped and does so with dismay
He gazes at me through quizzical eyes I wonder what he sees
An aunt who will adore him and give him everything to please.

R D Hiscoke

CHANGING SEASONS

It is definitely changing season time.
Summer makes room to the cooler autumn.
Bright colours die down and leave us with warm tones.
Leaves begin to fall and cover our paths
creating a delicate carpet.

It's that time of the year again.
Birds migrate to warmer climate.
Sunny days are more appreciated than ever.
When the sun is shining, we hurry out like lizards
to get a glimpse of it, like plants in need of light
for their survival.

Raining days are comforting as well.
They make you want to look at the world from the inside.
We find ourselves staring at the rain, dripping from the trees
and at the slow cars going by
and we can almost imagine hearing the windscreen wipers
moving from side to side.

The changing of the seasons is part of our perfect
synchronised world.

Welcome back autumn!

Franca Gatto

BANGKOK STREETS: A DESCRIPTION

Street stalls exhibiting
colourful trivia,
appetising delicacies,
bargaining opportunities,
nose-tickling aromas,
market din with waves of people,
the ebb and flow of traffic,
bubbling with transactions,
the occasional mini-skirted
lithe angel face.
Heat of day,
with watermelon to quench it,
iced soft drinks for dry throats,
as buses belch black exhaust fumes
and taxis tail each other.
The abundant enticing vitality
of Bangkok streets!
Skyscrapers nudging oriental bazaars,
glittering shrines and slummy side streets.
My footsteps get lost in the mazes;
What am I doing here?

Emmanuel Petrakis

THE BRIDEGROOM

A moment in church, I looked into his face,
What was he thinking? My son the bridegroom,
A quiet moment reflecting on his fate
Sitting in his chair, shadows of this wedding afternoon.

Later on the path around the churchyard,
His gasp of delight, for the scarlet tunics and the drums,
Posing with his bride before the Army Guard
Triumph for the 'secret' treat by his happy mum.

His speech was firm and well rehearsed
Until he spoke of his accident and to whom he owed his life
We gasped as he faltered and wept on fate or worse
But his father leapt up to grasp him and held him tight.

We spent the day in such moments, gulped and wept
Smiling and happy on a rollercoaster of alarms
End of the day, 'all's right' my son slept
With his carer, his wife, wrapped in her arms.

Lots has happened since disaster in Northern Ireland,
The helicopter ride home, hospitals and long nursing.
The highs were good and the lows often got out of hand
Today we had magic, the long awaited 'blessing'.

Forgive my indulgence, these tears are sheer joy
From nappy to rompers, jeans, a suit, the uniform
You caused me to swear, curse, scream and laugh bonny boy
You'll never behave and we are so glad you were born.

Jean Horsham

TABLETOP NAVY

When penny destroyers
with halfpenny submarines
plough through a tablecloth
all battles must end by teatime
ignoring signals
from a battleship
purchased from a wartime Woolworth's
all now in a tin box harbour
still carrying that musty smell
of old childhood.

Paul Wilkins

I'VE GOT TO DO IT

I've lived here now for forty years,
Lots of happiness and a few tears.
The time has come for me to go,
Yet where to move I just don't know.
The garden's too big and needs someone to care,
Now there's just me with no one to share.

I've been sorting things through in the loft today,
Old books and toys and games to play.
Lots of memories came flooding back,
I even found an old Santa sack.
I wonder why we hoard so much?
When it's out of sight it's out of touch.

I'll miss the view and glowing sunsets,
Leaving them behind with many regrets.
I'll miss friends and neighbours I've known for years,
We've helped one another through happiness and fears.
I'll miss the streets and familiar faces,
Soon I must make friends in other places.

A smaller place is what I need,
My inner voice I've got to heed.
With a heavy heart and tears of pain,
'I've got to do it,' I say once again.
But I'll always remember the happy times,
When I make the move to other climes.

Not long before I'm packed and gone,
Life is a challenge I'll meet it head on.
There'll be different streets and faces to see,
I wonder who my new neighbours will be?
For none of us know of the master plan,
But it's up to us to do the best we can.

Ruth Robinson

A SISTER'S LOVE
(Dedicated to Evelyn, my darling sister)

What's the benefit of a sister, some people may ask,
She's someone who'll help you whatever the task.
Growing up together, we had so much fun,
Long summer walks, or just lying in the sun.
If you do the dishes, then I'll make the bed,
No chance, I'd rather watch the TV instead.
Of course we would quarrel, sometimes even fight,
But we'd always make up before bedtime at night.
Sharing a room was sometimes a chore,
Especially you 'hanging' your clothes on the floor.
Looking back it seems only last year,
We lived together, these times I hold dear.
When you got engaged, everyone was glad,
Except for me, it just made me feel sad.
No one understood the pain I went through,
When I thought of you leaving, if only they knew.
The wedding was lovely, a beautiful bride,
On the arm of your father, faces covered with pride.
You moved into your new house, all happy and gay,
'Well, how's your sister?' people would say.
'Oh the house is lovely, there's not much to do'
And what about yourself? No word of you?
I miss you dear sister, since you moved out,
When you're in the area, give me a shout.
You know I love you, I always will,
I missed you then and I miss you still.

Joan Cardwell

MY ADOPTED DAUGHTER

I held you in my arms when you were one week old,
The child I had longed for, yet not my own.
Blue were your eyes and gold your hair,
I thought you beautiful beyond compare.

As tears of joy came with emotion,
I made a vow, which never was broken.
Our lives together we would always share,
I would stand beside you and always care.

You brought us joy beyond all measure,
Always for us our greatest treasure.
A bond which flourished through the years,
Giving us happiness and very few tears.

But now that I am old, in my 90th year,
It is to you I turn, my daughter dear,
For the strength and help to carry on,
Giving me love which is second to none.

No wonder I say to God above,
Thank you Lord for a daughter's love.

Phoenix

MY SISTER

Whose blue eyes
Full of surprise
Smile for me
Endlessly
My sister's

Whose loving face
And warm embrace
Holds me tight
Lovingly
My sister's

Whose endearing ways
Spread over days
Cares for me
Eternally
My sister's

Whose tearful smile
Waves goodbye awhile
Crying for me
Woefully
My sister's.

Margaret Gurney

LETTERS IN THE SAND

There are so many things in life
We'll never understand
Oh, fleeting are the joys of youth
Love letters in the sand.

The tides of life rush over them
Their fragile joy has gone,
Are blotted out, they are no more
And we are older grown.

But what is life without mistakes
By our mistakes we learn.
But do we want to be so learned,
When for our youth we yearn?

We may understand the meaning
Of all that has gone before,
But as the years keep rolling on
Opportunity comes no more
But the spectre of the Reaper
Comes nearer than before.

Oh! Could I go back to that youthful land
And live again those precious hours
And write again just one more time,
Those letters in the sand.

Isobel Laffin

I LOVE TO WATCH

As the winter's drawing in
And the ground begins to harden,
I love to watch the blackbirds,
As they search about the garden.
I give them all wild bird food,
Hang monkey nuts on the line,
I love to watch the blue tits,
As on the nuts they dine.
The robin comes to call each day,
He likes a bit of cheese,
He'll sit upon the fence and sing,
His way of saying please.
I love to watch the robin,
He listens - he's very wary,
I feed him lots of different things,
His diet - he likes to vary.
Once we had a greenfinch,
There was once a great tit too,
I love to watch the garden birds,
As they go about what they do.

Joyce Clegg

SPECIAL TIME

When Jesus came into my life
What joy it was for me
I felt such peace and happiness
It was my special time
I moved up to the Bible class
I learned more about my Saviour
And how our Saviour died for me.

Christmas Day 1932 I was baptised
I was 16 and now am 84
I still love my Saviour and friend
And still remember that wonderful day
On Jesus' birthday
I gave my heart to Him.

Gladys Bartley

FROLIC

Stanton Drew in Somerset
Is a frolic of lambs in a field of sleep.
It is older than time or tide and yet
Both are forgotten when young lambs leap
At Stanton Drew.

The Standing Stones are a testament
To pride and purpose of ages gone.
The strength outpoured, those millennia spent
On breaking rock for a shrine of stone
At Stanton Drew.

The lambs are tender and soon will grow
Out of this game of dancing grace -
One springtime festival - but now
They come full circle in this place
At Stanton Drew.

I shall never forget the lambs of the Stones
Signalling life at the start of the year,
Frolicking in a tumble of tones
Of white and grey - and a black is here -
To set you a scene to see life through
At Stanton Drew.

Joan Gordon

My Nanna

My nanna's eyes so blue and deep,
Would look at me while I would sit and weep,
A caring smile that would say,
Everything will be OK,
A cup of tea so sweet and hot,
Drank from a chipped pot,
A chocolate biscuit and the mantelpiece,
Waiting for the talking to cease,
The latest gossip she would tell,
Mostly of people unwell,
Family troubles and babies born,
The man next door finally cut his lawn,
My grampa she'd call him names,
But she loved him all the same,
When I told her a great gran she'd be,
Her arms she flung around me,
Tears of joy sprang to her eyes,
'Ei our Pamela what a surprise.'
A baby boy she held in her arms,
Pulled in by all his charms,
Four months later and so suddenly,
My nanna died and left me,
She comes to me in my dreams
And with a happy smile she beams,
'Please don't cry or be sad,'
She's having the best time she has ever had.

Pam Cook

THE FATHER'S DEAR ONES

Dear hearts, dear faces, dear lives -
Each soul, a glimpse of love,
To shine as a light from above,
Thought about with care -
Set apart, sanctified for eternity -
Unfettered by earthly circumstances,
Unrestricted by chains that seek to bind,
United by a simple wooden cross -
Out of time, out of space, out of step?
No - 'Go ye, where I place ye.' He said
Obediently each one lives,
Extending further still the bonds of love -
To be where He would have each one to be,
To bring His compassion, ultimately His joy -
Yet He can pluck them out of time, out of space,
Give them an awesome time of fellowship,
Years melt away to minutes, time stands still,
His family love bonds strengthened,
Hearts full of awe, because He restores bonds of love -
Time can't erode them, nor age, or infirmity decay them,
Distance can't separate souls -
A taste of time out of eternity, in heaven we'll party continually,
Redeemed, restored, renewed -
Created by a loving Father's heart!

Margi Hughes

CHRISTMAS CHILDHOOD MEMORY

When Christmas time it does arrive
Remembered from whenst a boy of five
Lay abed on Christmas Eve
So excited what Santa will leave.
Wide awake so as to see
What the red robed phantom will bring for me
Must have dozed off into slumber
Will he arrived at the right number?
The following morning early dawn
A young boy awoke with a yawn
Letting out a mighty scream
'Mummy, Mummy, Santa Claus has been'
Leaving parcels, boxes and assorted toys
Just one of Daddy's annual ploys.

Francis A Rawlinson

HOMESICK

Some of the happiest days of my life were fighting with that girl.
She would say one thing, I would shout another.
The argument would carry on,
Going round corners, crossing roads,
Turning back upon itself and eventually,
Eventually ending up somewhere neither of us had seen before.

We were happy exchanging pleasantries,
With our TV conversations.
Those were the happiest days of my life.
She gave me my sense of location and now I'm homesick.
I'm at the end of the line.
I mean, I've run out of puff and come to a gentle halt,
In the middle of nowhere.

Dawna-Mechelle Lewis

POET OF THE LAKES

My hobby
Is 'ever new'
Even though I have visited
More times than a few.
The lakes, the homes
And gardens
Of poet William Wordsworth.
A private man
Literary scholar
His books on verse
His life, in books.
Wonderful reading of the poet's 'world'
His ancestors, I have met
A joy, I will never forget.
In pride of place
A portrait of William Wordsworth
A treasured gift
Hangs on my wall.
I look for help
When poems I scrawl
And lines won't come at all.

Margaret Parnell

CHRISTMAS

Christmas Day 1999
Will be remembered
By my children, for laughter

Shared through generations,
Who together made it real

Here's to fairies, bingo and bins
New clothes, books
Laser guns and candles

Here's to you, my family and friends
Whose presence made the laughter possible

Michelle Howarth

MY CHILD

I held her in my arms, so close to my heart,
Soft and pink, a tiny bundle, a baby girl
My thoughts were heavy I felt no pain
Yet I knew in my heart we had to part.

The time had come, I had to hand her over
Motionless, not hearing the voices in my head
Murderous thought ticking over my brain
Right at that moment, I wished I was dead.

Then suddenly, like I was reborn again
I turned and ran, my baby held next to my heart
No one would take her, she'd always be mine
Together we'd go on to make a new start.

So all grown up, she lights up my life
No more pain, no more reason or rhyme
That day years ago that nearly ended in sorrow
Is a day of reflection, 'my very special time'.

E Corr

I HAVE A DREAM

I have a dream . . .

That in the future homelessness and hunger will be forgotten,
War and fighting will happen no more
And disease will be wiped out.
All dreams and hopes will be conquered.
People will help others whatever their needs
And all the time words will be used like 'thank you' and 'please'.
All countries will come together to prevent global warming,
Murders and crimes of all sorts will disappear.
There would be no more forest fires
And animals won't lose their habitat.
Senseless killing of animals would be yesterday's news
And winners won't laugh in front of those that lose.
I hope in the future Girl Guides and Scouts will be full up
And people won't be obsessed with money and greed,
So the rich can help those people in need.
Schools would put a stop to bullying
So fights would be abandoned, like kicking and hair pulling.
Everyone would have a perfect pet and wild animals would run free.

That is my dream.

Melanie Derbyshire

GRANDMA

You're going to be a grandma,
What a lovely glow that brings,
The chuckles of a baby
And baby clothes and things.

To have this magic all again,
My head goes in a whirl,
Will my darling little grandchild,
Be a little boy or girl.

To rub the bumps and bruises,
When they're learning how to walk,
The gabbles and the splutters,
When they're learning to talk.

To see the wonder in the eyes,
That see a dog or cat,
The puzzled look that clearly says,
'I wonder what was that.'

Robert Simpson

LITTLE ANGELS

An angel, a cherub, a sleeping child
Or maybe two,

Can be found in the Old Masters'
Paintings and sculptures too.

But in real life you can still see
Them embodied here,

For they exist in all little children
Far and near.

If you are fortunate enough to have
Children yourself,

You'd have seen often your child asleep
Innocence itself.

Who has not crept into the room at night
To take a peep

And stopped to admire them laying
In sleep so deep.

So peaceful, quiet, clean and beautiful
Such a setting.

A reminder of angels and cherubs,
Of the paintings.

Terry Daley

A Gift

Having children is a gift not everybody has,
It's special and not something you can buy or be given by anybody,
You get a tiny, cute, bundle of joy that takes over your life forever.

You worry, cry, love and watch over them all the time,
It's like a permanent 24 hour job but instead of getting paid in money,
You get paid in love.

As they grow older, you can never remember what it was like
For them not to be around,
They become a part of you forever.

Anna Lourensz

OH MIRACLE SEED OF LIFE

Our love then shone in the night
to introduce, so bright - another light

for I need to say today
two hundred and eight days away

its joyous news I'll say
an acknowledgement on this day

for all our pain inside
from that we'll never hide

both left alone and so young
now brought together made as one
and now a new life has begun

deep within delicate walls so thin
crown our side of life to live

more precious than mountains of gold
diamonds - coins of old

into the future she comes at last
no more a seed entombed in the past

so proud I began to cry
even gave her a tear from my eye

I count your fingers and little toes
feel your hair, touch your nose
you're a perfect daughter - God rightly knows

miracle of God's creation - ever so close to perfection
mirrored image of my own reflection

Graham Hare

ANNA'S BIBLE

Today I introduced her
to the one
she danced with yesterday
and in doing so
made him a stranger.

Yesterday she ran around
screaming her incoherent prayers
that brought pleasure to her God
and in doing so
made me happy.

Today she has words,
stories, names of kings and inconsequential heroes.
Where did I ever get the idea
that words can improve
on what you have when you are three?

Yesterday they were one.
Today I gave her the map
that will eventually lead her back
to yesterday.
and in doing so
broke my own heart.

Henry Birtley

MY LITTLE ONE

Blonde hair, blue eyes, fair skin,
You are a delight,
All through the day and all through the night,
You are our son and we love you,
Your dad and I,
How come we have been blessed,
We ask ourselves why?

What have we done in our lives,
To enable us to have someone like you,
We are most grateful,
That you are you.

So playful and bright,
But full of mischief too,
You are indeed our little boy
In grown up shoes.

What will we do when you have grown,
We hope you are the same little boy,
From the same little town,
With the values we have taught you,
We hope you will recall,
When you change to a man from a little boy.

Whatever you choose to do in your life,
Your dad and I will be there to make
Everything alright.

Jill K Gilbert

CHILDREN - LISTEN!

Children are our future -
    Yes, that's been said before,
But, listen to our children
    And open up the door.
If you really listen
    Then, you will hold the key;
For, they're tomorrow's people
    Affecting you and me.
Don't fob them off 'Yes, later dear'
    Their problem's real, now, true.
So, listen, know them, *hear*
    What 'future' holds for you!

Pat Rapley

THE FIRST TIME

The first time
That she smiles at you
The first word
That she speaks
Her growing years
The learning phase
The joy you feel unique
You teach her, guide her
Through those days
Her growing years soon fly
She then becomes a teenager
And always questions why
Before long she wears make-up
Then student days are here
You feel as proud as you can be
A woman she appears
She's grown into a beauty now
A certain grace you see
You've taught her well
This child of yours
How much she has achieved.

Jeanette Gaffney

REFLECTIONS
(For Ben)

There are means to hear a mind
develop fantastic fears -
my ears are filled with goblins!

However, (I am told)
it's the fairy folk who paint
those pictures in our sleep.

My eyes delight
at the scampering
words from his mouth,

frivolous smiles
in a totter
to Wonderland.

Today reveals a boy
the image of his father,
once upon a time.

Douglas W Gray

MARION

Marion's thirty-one now, has grown away
Yet I still remember that August day
Thrashing around, my head a whirl
As mighty pushes brought forth a girl
At nine months old Marion walked unaided
And as she grew, her blonde hair faded
Marion was never naughty, a model child
Quiet her nature, so meek and mild
Playing the recorder, violin as well
Many memories fade, it's so hard to tell
Looking back to then, what would she be
Marion so like her daddy with only scrapes of me
My darling girl with that sparkling bright face
Who made our home such a happy place
How proud we were of our lovely child
With her bonny face, the way she smiled
Watching my daughter grow like a blossoming tree
With bits of her daddy, just little bits of me
Then one day this young man came
Asking for her hand, and to share his name
As I watched new life grow within my life
For my Marion had become both mother and wife
Giving birth to her own bundle of joy
My first grandchild, a dear little boy
Into the world my sweet Marion came
My own little girl with her unique name
Years pass and our memories often stray
But I'll never forget that warm August day
So remember Marion from whence you began
And that other special person, and who I am.

Ann Hathaway

BEING HONEST

I found a ring in my street,
It was just underneath the seat.
I took it to the police station,
So they could start an investigation.

They asked me where I found the ring,
I said 'By a seat so I brought it in.'
After three months the police phoned me,
And told me whose ring it would be.

A day or two later I received a letter,
With a reward that couldn't be better,
The lady was pleased with what I had done,
For being honest, I told my mum.

Eileen Denham

CHILDREN

The joys that children bring are numerous and diverse.
Daily events can be funny, but can often make you curse.
One thing's for certain after the birth of your child,
The feelings you experience are strong, never mild.
You become a provider who is always there,
Giving loving attention and twenty-four hour care.
Times can be hard when tiredness sets in.
When there's squabbles and screams, and uncontrolled din.
Gladly these times are sporadic and few.
Most days give you pleasure, after a game or two.
Watching them grow into a little person with views.
Coming home from school, full of stories and news.
Learning together is a delight, not a chore.
Sadly the results may mean you have to do more.
Go forward together, support as they grow.
Be not just a parent, but a friend who does know.
Protect all you can, but do not hinder their life.
Their life is for living, if you restrict, there's strife.
Discuss options, don't let tempers flare.
Mutual respect will prevent, or make upsets rare.
Being a parent makes you truly blest.
The emotions within really are the best.
Love so deep and so hard to explain.
When your child is away, the loss causes you pain.
You want the best, that's all you strive for.
A happy child, who could ask for more?

Anne Sackey

THE NEW ARRIVAL

'It's a girl,' he said,
Such joy, such pride.
His sheer delight -
He could not hide.

'She's red and wrinkled,
With bright blue eyes.'
Both parents have brown,
So it's quite a surprise.

She has jet-black hair
Far more than her dad.
He was bald as a babe,
And quite blond as a lad.

Eight little fingers,
Two thumbs and ten toes.
And ev'rything else -
Is complete, I suppose.

'She's perfect' he crowed.
Well, what else would she be?
This darling new grandchild -
To bounce on my knee.

Anne M Jones

PAINTING WALLS

Always,
at some point,
when I paint a wall
I think of you
when you were very small -
three, or four,
no more.

The adjoining wall,
the dining room,
in Meadow Lane
where, as I painted,
in you came,
in your mouth
a biro pen
and then,
as you peered into the tin
and opened up your mouth to speak
the pen fell in
and sank beneath
. . .
You looked at me,
I looked at you,
we didn't speak,
you went away.

And now you paint as well as I did then
but sometimes I wonder,
whatever happened to that pen?

Ian Metcalfe

MY METAMORPHIC CHILD

Is this angelic, sleeping child the same being
       who drove me wild today?
This child, who awoke me at dawn,
       persistently demanding to play.
Such sweet innocence, quietly breathing,
       all youthful energy expended;
Inquisitive mind resting, eyelids tightly closed,
       exuberant voice silent.
What dreams are you dreaming this night?
My sweet metamorphic child.

M Andrews

DAUGHTER

You're my baby
I used to say
I watched you grow
Day after day
You've made me laugh
You've made me cry
And then I looked around
And you were five

Now from five to fifteen
And all those years in-between
Life wasn't plain sailing
I wish it had been
But now you've reached twenty
And a woman 'you are now'
And the mother that loved you then
Still loves you now.

Helen McAlinden

TIME TRAVEL

A score of years and more dissolved
when your bright eyes peered into mine,
as if there and then it was resolved
that our hearts should intertwine.

Sweet mirror image of my gem,
you melted into anxious arms,
wearing her looks like a diadem,
crushing my lungs with your charms.

Caitlin, you're so much like her when
forty was oh, so old to me.
I'm here for you now, and will be then -
though I twice that age might be.

Perry McDaid

YESTERDAY!

In my little garden
I sat under a green tree
I looked up
The fowls of the air
Lodged in the branches
Oh, what a beauty
A wonderful light to behold
Before mine eyes
The birds danced
Among the branches
While I gazed at nature
I thought about the Maker
Who provides for the raven his food
When his young ones cry unto God.

Ebenezer Essuman

DAUGHTERS

My daughters, I have three,
Like stepping stones, you came to me,
One, two, three, upon my knee,
Dark hair, and fair,
Such a mix of little girls
Some with straight hair
Some with curls,
Growing lovely every day
Soon to be grown up, going away.
My heart aches to see you go
But one, two, three,
It was so.
You fell in love
It was time to leave,
I watched you go, my heart on my sleeve.
No longer mine
But always in my heart you'll shine
Beloved always, and yes,
        Still mine!

Doreen Ellen Thomson

FIRST-BORN CHILD

I remember when my first-born
Was just a little child,
Chubby cheeks and golden hair -
Innocence undefiled.

Such a lovely little girl
(Though oft-times rather shy)
With her growing mind inquiring
She was always asking 'Why?'

Then we'd try to tell her,
In words she'd understand,
How the wonders of the universe
Were formed by God's own hand.

We used to have our cuddle times
And include her little brother,
Or I would sit and read to her -
Then she'd listen to her mother.

But everything must have its day
And childhood must come to pass.
From a tiny babe in arms
She's become a fine young lass.

When I see her standing tall
My heart fills with pride and love.
My daughter - O my daughter,
A gift from God above.

Marian J Dunham

To Raise A Child

From the cradle to a tiny tot,
through the terrible two's,
through all their 'I will nots',
and all their 'Can I do's?'
From a toddler to a teen,
and all the years in-between.
Tantrums and testing times,
finding out who is the boss,
but we go on loving them
good or bad because,
they bring us joy and pleasure,
and memories to treasure,
they supply us with a talking point,
and help to eat the Sunday joint.
We guide them and we teach them
what is right and wrong,
always reassuring them, home is where
we all belong.
No one is perfect, but if we do our very best,
we will have helped to raise a child,
a child who has respect.
A baby sent from heaven above,
is meant to have a lot of love,
with maternal patience and lots of affection,
we do our best to create perfection.

Audrey Taylor

MISSING VOICES

It's rarely heard, the joyful sound,
Of children hard at play.
Skipping, jumping, screaming,
Or the lesser game of hopscotch.
They have forgotten how to play

Instead they find to occupy their time,
Saga and Nintendo skilled crafted games.
In front of the console their lives are changed,
They grunt and groan and weird faces make.

When they are unable to reach the levels,
Or master another game.
In increasing circles their lives rotate,
When the games take control.

Simple pleasures of group play forgotten,
But happy voices squeal within.
They brag and boast to their mates,
How skilful they have become.

Where has the joy of laughter gone?
For it is rarely heard.

Joseph Barrow

A TREASURE

A longed-for arrival, a bundle of joy
No special wishes for a girl or boy.
Parents and relatives gather their love to employ
And toast the event with champagne, to enjoy.

A cute little baby, sparkling eyes and fair hair
A treasure to hold, and such love to share
With ten little fingers and ten little toes
A delicate skin, and a pert little nose.

Three years will pass and time for school
With tumbling curls and a packed lunch the rule
The joy of learning to embrace and share
Such fun and laughter, and learning to care.

As time goes by, there will be, interests galore
Dancing, swimming, games and so much more
Not forgetting a guide to character and all
No matter how developing, in statue, short or tall

So teenage years arrive, a difficult time
With the future ahead, in which to shine
An answer to parents, and relations alike
For guiding and loving, the success they would like.

C King

GEMMA WORLD

It's a long way to the bottom stair it seems
As Gemma wanders down
Light dances upon the wooden beams
And gives Gemma a golden crown
So she can pretend she's a princess fair.
But breakfast is ready and shopping to be done
With the help of Mr Teddy Bear.
Rainy days are best for puddles are fun.
Hope we go to the park again.
Push me on the swings high.
Now I can count to ten.
Time to go, their sweeties to buy
And shoes to try on smart and new.
Then I'll choose pretty ribbons in my hair to tie
To match my dress of blue.
Just like holidays so nice
With sticky rock, yellow sand and sea,
Tiny grains always stick to my toes like rice.
Licking ice-cream cones is lovely
This is happiness.
Just like birthdays and growing up tall.
And digging in the garden for worms is best.
Put on yellow wellingtons kept by the door.
Such muddy hands and face all grin.
Tea's ready, bedtime not far away
Out with the storybook now I begin.
But Gemma, eyes are closing after her busy day.

M Hanmer

A DAWN EXPERIENCE . . . STONEHENGE 1981

I felt a mystic pull of magic and overwhelming awe,
as I was drawn, impelled closer to those mysterious pointing stones.
Suddenly this world silenced, and I was transported to a lost,
but vividly real world - somewhere else - perhaps in times past.
A place of which a spirituality now lies, buried in deep denizens
of our minds.
I breathed a sweet clean air, that whistled in seeming time-winds
that blew . . .
Carrying those silent secrets which I could almost hear.
Voices of a people long ago, yet very close now.
A pulse of exultation, wild and lovely burst in me, as staring
heavenwards, into the glowing coloured eye of dawn -
I touched the shadowed stones, and felt something . . .
Incredibly ancient, seemingly timeless even; like an unconscious
meaning brimming almost to the shore of conscious realisation.
A feeling never felt before.
Awe streamed like adrenaline, surging through me as I made contact
with the monolithic monument and romanced back, across the
vault of time.
Swallowed by thoughts, I yielded to the dream - real forces and
envisioned images of lost truths of what has been . . .
and invisibly is still.
Strange deep emotions ran in me. It was like an encounter with all the
elements of creation. A return of a part of me unseen, hidden a sense of
wonderment.
A oneness, a bond and union of body and soul.
It was as if time itself, trembled and changed within that circle.
Twilight faded into the drifting white ground mists, as dawn's vibrant
coloured onslaught came, diminishing the remnant stars overhead.
Warm sunbeams broke free of the banks of slowly receding purple
clouds on the horizon.

Paul Holland

MY EYES

For years I have lived,
With eyes that did not see,
Only a little,
Not properly.

Now medical science
Has changed that for me,
My sight is restored,
And now I can see
Not just a little
But properly.

My thick glasses have gone
No longer required.
Though part of me
For seventy years
Now they have gone
I am not shedding tears.

It is so wonderful
Now I can see
The beauty that surrounds me
I also see my wrinkled face,
And dust and dirt
All over the place.

Irene Millington

FEBRUARY 1944

It was February 1944:
I lay asleep in my Nissen Hut
At El Gamil, the airport near Port Said,
Dreaming no doubt of my wife and home
And baby boy, when suddenly someone
Was shaking me . . .
Shaking and shoving
In violent excitement
And shouting in a sort of hoarse
Strangulated whisper:
'Bill,' he said, 'Bill, it's me,
Dave from the office,
Bill, wake up, you've got a Blighty posting!
It's just come through;
It's not a joke, Bill, it's true,
You lucky sod,
It's a named posting, Bill,
Back to Blighty,
Your name is on it, name and number,
All correct
As God's my judge I swear it.'

That was more than fifty years ago,
But I must have relived that moment
Fifty thousand times or so.

William R Braide

ENTERING THE CAWOOD ART FESTIVAL

I entered the annual Cawood Festival of Art,
It's in August keeping July and September apart;
I travelled in the car and carried Ben,
To the church we went, the promise broken.
I parked the car and entered the church,
On a wall near me was a perch;
It was a drawn picture of a fish,
On a table was money in a dish.
I saw busy Dot, she recognised me too,
She asked what I had, it was new;
I gave her the Space Station written project,
She had no intention to offer me reject.
I offered her payment, she said, 'Forget it,'
The judges were judging, I gave a bit;
I was a regular entry whom people knew,
No entry form or name was needed - too.
I was a day late, people don't mind,
I'm an entertainer, I would please the blind;
I went back to the car and disappeared,
I thought to myself,
'Winning's possible and weird.'
I have a Bachelor of Arts Honours degree,
Fine Art's my subject, you have to agree;
I've done some painting, two-one's my score,
Inside and outside of buildings is even more.
I've prepared to work for family and friends,
It's gone onto decoration for earning money trends;
Being an artist exhibiting his pieces to sell,
Has no future and makes a loss's hell.

Ian K A Ferguson

RECOLLECTIONS OF THE CAMBRIAN

(Cambrian refers to the Cambrian Railways Company,
Wales' largest independent railway company)

Speed and splendour was the age
To travel by rail was all the rage
From sheep and milk to coal and steels
On iron rails went metal wheels
With plume of smoke and company crest
Each company boasted they're the best
But alas the splendid age has died
And between the tracks the weeds abide.

With deserted buildings and platforms empty lie
Whilst the Home and Distant point silently to the sky
Here vandals take their toll
Where mighty engines used to roll
Familiar cries 'All change I say'
To so-called progress have given way
Now ivy climbs the station house
The home of giants now hides a mouse

The engine sheds once the scene of pride
Like the signal box, derelict by the side
The station clock still points to four
Beneath this lies an open door
The booking office and waiting room
Depict a scene of awful gloom
And train departures on the wall begin to fade
And paintwork turns a thousand shades

With broken windows and fallen fence
This future to me makes no sense
And as nature takes over
The permanent way grows clover
With sleepers all gone and relics so few
Am I dreaming or is this true?

The past recalls a scene of delight
Of passengers and goods through until twilight
The smell of gas, engine oil and the sight of steam
Of morning mail, papers and fish and dairy cream
And stations and staff all smart and clean
Oh, better days are those I have seen.

Malcolm Douglass

DEBBIE AND MARTIN'S DAY

October 9th 1999, we spoke our precious vows and became
One, united by our golden bands of pure love.
My heart was beating with nerves and excitement at being
Watched by our family and friends as we exchanged
Our words of commitment, love and fidelity.
'Something old' was my favourite black velvet frock jacket.
'Something new' was my shimmering silver silken dress.
'Something borrowed' was Michelle's amber ring.
'Something blue' was hidden from view!
We grinned at each other in joy and held back tears of love
As we stood together, looking at one another and spoke
Our special words. The moment we exchanged our
Golden rings was a gesture of eternity, never-ending love.
When the Registrar spoke, saying 'Mr and Mrs Perks'
I felt so proud and happy to be your wife.
I will love and protect you, Martin, throughout my life.
I love you always.

Debbie Perks

ISAIAH 60 V 1

('Arise, shine for your light has come and
the glory of the Lord is risen upon you')

The Spirit says rise up and shine
Awaken from your sleep
Your healing comes on eagle's wings
As deep speaks unto deep

Don't look for me outside yourself
For I will be found within
For in the place where you were formed
You were despised and scorned

But for your life I had a plan
A place for my creation
For you my child are precious
And there will be no separation

The seed that sits within you
And lies there null and void
Will be brought back to life
As my spirit heals your soul

You will break forth and blossom
A flower of rare beauty
My child just sit and love me
Don't do it as a duty

Your love means so much more to me
Than any work you do
So let us spend some time together
No one else, just me and you.

Ann Langley

A Dawn Bolero

Slowly, dreamily;	First Voice:	Morning in the City,
Reply, muted;	Second Voice:	Morning in the City,
	First Voice:	The light comes flooding from the east,
		And every court and stair and alley,
		Glows with the swelling day's increase.
		Morning in the City,
	Second Voice:	Morning in the City -
		Aurora steps with feet of gold,
		And from her skirts the photons sparkle
		Advancing with the dawn's threshold.
	Both Voices	Morning in the City.
Tempo increases	First Voice:	Now comes the rattle of the milk float,
		The postman with purposeful tread,
		The women start to bustle breakfast,
		And rouse the children from their bed.
Staccato;	Second Voice:	Now comes the car, the bus, the lorry,
		The City wakens with a roar,
	Both Voices:	The office lights pale in the sunlight,
		The presses start on fact'ry floor.
		We are not ready with maxims,
		And our opinion's rarely sought,
		But without us there is no city,
Crescendo;		No pot is thrown, no pattern wrought.
Moderato;	First Voice:	Morning in the City!
Muted reply;	Second Voice:	Morning in the City.

N R Worrall

Congratulations On Attaining Your Nurse Practitioner Degree, *Amanda.*

The ladder of success, you've climbed,
With great determination,
And culled rewards - you so deserve,
For all the preparation
Involved in training to achieve,
Your final validation.

I'm really proud that you are part
Of our Institution,
And wish you well in all you do,
With every realisation,
And finally I forecast this
Complete personification.

Good luck
      and
           Good health

                Love Bett

Elizabeth Jones (Betty)

FINAL DAY

I rise for a final time from this bed.
I am in my parents' home.
I prepare,
Collecting the items I need for my departure.
Preparing my face and body for
People's amusement and disgust.

Stepping into the shower I see
Something I shouldn't.
A picture of my betrothed and I
In an old black and white photo booth.
It sits discarded, lodged between
The shower and sink unit.
I step out and wonder
If my decision is right.

No turning back now,
The decision is made.

Tenderly I kiss the retrieved photograph.
Preparing never to see the boy
Portrayed here again.
I take the creams, rubbing them in,
Looking at my perfectly prepared body
In readiness for this day.

I am ready, the time has come.
Collecting the final items
I retire from my chamber,
As I hear my mother approaching.
Taking with me, something old,
Something new, something borrowed,
And something blue.

Giselle Ni Riain

TEACHER'S PETS

Dorothy sent a photo to the Derbyshire Times
Of her class in 1960. Four rows of children
Five or six years old, who listened to nursery rhymes,
Fairy stories, the percussion band. Hair tied with ribbon,
Plaid skirts, short trousers, thirty pupils each with a happy face
Seventeen absentees had measles. Among my souvenirs
A gift from one child has pride of place
For this was my class in later years.
Yesterday's children are middle-aged
In this millennium year. Dorothy is ninety.
I'm a pensioner remembering concerts we staged,
Sports Day fun, classroom pets, morning Assembly,
The headmistress's painted nails on the piano keys,
Mrs Cooke making films on Saturday mornings,
The long walk to the canteen in winter's frost and freeze.
We had a library, a French room, a kiln, museum paintings.
Ralph, the caretaker, helped with Christmas decoration.
Valerie taught in the partially-hearing unit.
Rounders in the park, dinner money and registration,
Wet playtimes, milk and biscuits, a lost PE kit,
Reading in groups, counting in fives,
So the cycle of the year ran its course.
I can now but speculate whether these lives
Are still interwoven. In honest discourse,
In dreams or meditation do yesterday's children
Sometimes recall our happy times? Do they
At the school gates reminisce in conversation
As they watch grandchildren at play?
I wonder how they fared in forty years
Learning life's lessons in laughter and tears.

Vivienne Brocklehurst

SIMPLICITY

A child's smile lights up the room
A cheeky grin relieves the gloom.
They have no fear when making friends,
Have the funniest ways to make amends.
If others upset through thoughtlessness
They are quick to forgive and court no fuss.
Living in a world that is free from care
Where all regardless are welcome there.

All it needs is make-believe
A concept we adults find hard to achieve.
An empty pot is poured with care
Into a cup that holds nothing but air,
The cup is held and sipped with glee
And make-believe biscuits are eaten for tea.
What more could they want? Nothing, I feel!
It's just the way they are, it is *not* unreal.

Tireless beings? Perhaps from outer space,
Never phased when they fall from grace.
Each angel contains a mischievous child
Full of fun, yet meek and mild.
To them life is simply meant for living
That's why they are always loving and giving.
Yes . . . a child's smile is a joy to behold
Costing nothing! Worth its weight in gold!

Gwyneth Wynn Davies

THE JOY OF CHILDREN

(For Colin and David - a mother to her sons)

Do you think of who you came from
Of what you came to be?
Do you ever ponder what life might have been
If one person had been different, one decision had been changed,
Would you be the men you are, or your lives be rearranged?
Could your mother or your father have been better in some ways?
Would you be the person in the way you are today?
In all the years I have known you,
In all the times we shared,
Did you always spare a thought inside for those
                                who loved and cared?
Years are five and twenty since you came into my world,
To me, my life, my history, before me was unfurled.
When you my sons were born to me,
More precious jewels I would never see.
Through any pain and misery,
My life shone through your smiling eyes,
Mother's love that never dies.
Sometimes happy, sometimes tears,
For five and twenty changing years.

Anne Marie Birley

JOLLY JUVENILES!

Seen kids on computers, inquiring of tutors,
And keen to press each button and each key?
Gosh! They're so excited! Thrilled to bits! Delighted!
What joy to see their faces full of glee!

Intense and so involved, until a problem's solved,
And then they'll look around for something more!
They're never satisfied, yet fill your heart with pride!
They're all enthusiastic to the core!

Of course, they make mistakes, and cause a few heartaches!
And yet they're quick to learn and eager, too!
Each sits with winning smile! Determined to beguile!
They'll charm you till you've done what you must do!

You'll buy new 'stuff' each month, then sit and read the 'bumph'
And then you'll do your best to 'sort it out'!
'Hopefully . . .' it works right - with everyone polite!
For that is what the family's all about!

Great, you've done your duty! 'Fixed the little beauty!'
Rejoice when one and all are feeling glad!
Soon as the gizmo's done, then folks start having fun!
'Gosh, that's flippin' marv'llous! Brilliant, Dad!!'

Thank God you saved some cash! Stored in your secret 'stash'!
Today your kids admit you've done your best!
'Dad, here's your cup of tea!' Good God, they all agree!
Praise God with hallelujahs you're so blessed!!

Denis Martindale

JOY OF CHILDREN

Joy to the world
A child is born
From flesh too solid
Joy at being born

Praise to the Lord
The Earth is ours
Worldwide joy at new life
Equal in the eyes of God

Long may you reign
Over the world with health
Independent thinker a curse
On the life you spawn

Softly out into the night
Nearby children fight
Was it English you spoke?
Presence is welcome here

For joy in being born
Look back at the man behind you
He carries a bomb
Women hold a banner

What to do with the children?
Do what you did before
Teach the children words
Get them when they are young

Best of the six top of the class
Crowds push surge forward
To catch a glimpse of the children
Children our place in the future
Sounds in the street of laughter
Some weeping, some singing of songs.

S M Thompson

SUBMISSIONS INVITED
SOMETHING FOR EVERYONE

POETRY NOW 2001 - Any subject,
any style, any time.

WOMENSWORDS 2001 - Strictly women,
have your say the female way!

STRONGWORDS 2001 - Warning!
Age restriction, must be between 16-24,
opinionated and have strong views.
(Not for the faint-hearted)

All poems no longer than 30 lines.
Always welcome! No fee!
Cash Prizes to be won!

Mark your envelope (eg *Poetry Now) 2001*
Send to:
Forward Press Ltd
Remus House, Coltsfoot Drive,
Peterborough, PE2 9JX

**OVER £10,000 POETRY PRIZES
TO BE WON!**

Judging will take place in October 2001